Compassionate Teaching inspires an authentic dialogue concerning first-generation college students' success and the barriers both faculty and students face. Amelia Leighton Gamel acknowledges and shares hard truths about her experience teaching first-generation, marginalized college students and the "how" behind the negative cycles she broke that increased her students' success. This book will change classroom dynamics if change is the true desire.

–LaShonda B. Fuller, Ph.D., Faculty Specialist
at Western Michigan University

In a time where access to post-secondary education is offered, in theory, to all and retention tactics remain the topic of conversation in regard to student success, Gamel's book brings to the forefront the need for an educational facelift starting with those in positions of power, authority, and privilege.

–Dr. LaSonda Wells, LPC, NCC, Counselor Educator,
Owner of Restorative Solutions Counseling and Consulting

Amelia Leighton Gamel's latest work goes to the heart of the cultural and context issues that contribute to equity gaps for first-generation students. It is powerful, insightful and focused on strategies and approaches that change the classroom and student success dynamic.

–Diane K. Troyer, Ph.D., Achieving the Dream Leadership Coach

COMPASSIONATE
TEACHING

COMPASSIONATE
TEACHING

UNLOCKING THE POTENTIAL
OF **FIRST-GENERATION**
MARGINALIZED STUDENTS

AMELIA LEIGHTON GAMEL

Visit the author's website at www.equitableedu.org.

ISBN: 9781725883253

Cover Photo © Stan Gaz

Printed in the United States of America

CONTENTS

PREFACE

The past several years has seen a concerted effort to increase the number of first-generation, low-income, and marginalized students in institutes of higher education. Getting students registered and in the door is one thing; keeping them there is another. The Postsecondary National Policy Institute reports that just 11 percent of low-income students who are the first in their family to attend college will have a college degree within six years of enrolling in school.

Colleges have responded to bleak retention and persistence rates by implementing a host of interventions, from creating streamlined program pathways, to implementing student success initiatives, to reformatting or eliminating remedial classes altogether. Although these interventions are well-intended and even promising, they don't address what often is a core factor in the students' success—or lack of success—at the institution: their relationship to the classroom environment.

First-generation, marginalized students who find themselves on campuses of predominately white institutions are often sensitive to signals that suggest, or are interpreted as, racial bigotry or intolerance. Such perceptions can easily make students feel like unwelcome outsiders in the classroom, increase their anxiety, and impact their sense of belonging—all of which can contribute to failing grades, subsequent loss of financial assistance, and withdrawal from the institution.

Even without the added burden of feeling like outsiders, students of color often are educated in under-resourced K-12 systems and are less academically prepared for college-level work. For marginalized young people *with* a degree, garnering employment that provides a living wage can be challenging; garnering employment that provides a living wage *without* a degree is nearly impossible.

It's sometimes difficult to separate the experiences, challenges, and needs of one student group from those of another. For example, the Pell Institute reports that first-generation college students are disproportionately minorities from low-income backgrounds and that nearly 30 percent are from families with an annual income less than $25,000.

Although educational attainment won't solve all issues related to equity, economic and otherwise, post-secondary achievement is a lifeline for many. This book is a response to my desire for equity that not only gives marginalized students opportunities to access education and economic stability, but intentionally and purposefully insists on it. It is meant as a call for action among my colleagues in higher education to rethink the college classroom environment and the critical role faculty members play in engaging and interacting with first-generation, marginalized students.

My inspiration comes directly from my students. I know what likely will happen to them if they don't persist and earn their degrees, but I also know how much they will flourish if they have the resources and supports they need to complete post-secondary education.

The information presented in this book is a culmination of my reading and study as well as my observations and experiences while growing up in a single parent, low-income home, attending public schools with significant populations of under-resourced students, being a first generation college student, teaching first-generation, marginalized college students from urban areas and advocating for underserved, under-resourced young men in the judicial system.

While doing research for my master's thesis paper, which discussed vocabulary acquisition strategies among community college developmental education students, I stumbled upon data about the reading levels of incarcerated African American men. At that time, I was spending a significant amount of time at the local courthouse observing hearings, arraignments, and other court proceedings. I also was reading Michelle Alexander's book *The New Jim Crow*, in which she addresses the mass incarceration of African-American men.

My research and observations shed new light on the concept of the school-to-prison pipeline as well as the correlation between illiteracy and incarceration. I quickly realized what would likely befall my African-American college students who weren't reading at grade level. I could almost see how their lives were likely to play out without academic readiness: failing grades, deflating self-esteem, dropping out, under- or unemployment, lifelong economic struggle, and for some, incarceration. That realization had a powerful impact on my teaching and inspired me to search for ways to create change.

A few years after earning my master's degree, I founded Men of Merit (MoM) for college men and Sisters of Strength (SoS) for college women— two campus initiatives that promoted the success and advancement of African-American college students. That experience allowed me to see that a different outcome was possible. Through rapport with and among the students, weekly meetings, powerful discussions, courageous conversations, monthly inspirational speakers, and a fostering of brotherhood and sisterhood, most of the students persisted from semester to semester; many graduated with their associate's degree and several went on to earn bachelor's and master's degrees. For those who weren't able to complete, I am still hoping for their return to higher education.

While there is no universally accepted definition, this book will define a first-generation student as a college student whose parents have not earned a college degree. And although first-generation, marginalized students from under-resourced areas vary in race and ethnicity and the strategies in this book are appropriate for all students, it should be noted that my reading, research, observations, experiences, and interactions have largely included African-American students and thus will be the focus of my writing throughout.

This book will:

- Shed light on the causative factors that drive self-sabotaging student behaviors.
- Explore students' beliefs, attitudes, and values.
- Encourage faculty to explore their core beliefs, attitudes, and behaviors.
- Encourage faculty to understand, anticipate, and empathically respond to students' behaviors.
- Provide strategies to build community and develop rapport with and among first-generation, marginalized students.

I've included real-life classroom stories to illustrate the self-sabotaging behaviors that students sometimes rely on to navigate life and education systems. Please note the names of the students have been changed to protect their identities.

As you read this book and think about the plight of first-generation, marginalized students, I hope you will realize how much is at stake not only for them, but also for their families and our communities.

I invite you to respond to this call for action and join me in rethinking the classroom experience and the critical role faculty have in the success and advancement of first-generation, marginalized students.

May you come away from this book with an energized passion for compassionate teaching that embraces first-generation, marginalized students and a resolve for their degree attainment.

ACKNOWLEDGMENTS

First, I would like to thank my husband, Kiernan, for his unwavering support, understanding, and acceptance of my commitment to first-generation, marginalized students. I will be forever grateful for his willingness to spend hours listening to my stories, previewing my chapters, and sharing his expertise in human behavior and social work. Without him, this book would not have been possible.

I would also like to thank Kimberly Cutting, my most dear and loyal friend, who on a daily basis engages in conversation with me regarding everything related to race, equity, and privilege. Even though it's more my fight than hers, she's right there by my side fighting the battle with me.

Although it would be impossible to name all the students who have been integral to my learning and understanding of the first-generation African-American experience, I would like to specifically thank Victor and Victoria Short, Darius McCarty-Hodges, and Deangelo Hawkins-Clay. My deepest gratitude goes to the original members of the Men of Merit and Sisters of Strength who were more like sons and daughters than students and who left indelible marks on my life. I would also like to thank the students' families who welcomed me into their lives and shared with me the pride, happiness, and concern of having a first-generation son, daughter, grandson or granddaughter.

Many thanks to my friend and colleague, Dr. Candy McCorkle, Vice President for Diversity and Inclusion at Western Michigan University, who continues to help me understand equity, social justice, and privilege.

I am sincerely grateful for my editors, Patricia George and Kat Groshong, who were integral in this book coming to fruition. Special thanks to Kat for the book cover design and text formatting.

I would like to thank Stan Gaz for the front cover photo.

Finally, I'd like to thank Dr. Diane K. Troyer, Achieving the Dream Leadership Coach and Dr. LaSonda Wells, LPC, NCC, Counselor Educator, Owner of Restorative Solutions Counseling and Consulting for their support, feedback, and endorsement. I would especially like to thank Dr. LaShonda B. Fuller, Ph.D., Faculty Specialist at Western Michigan University for her feedback, contribution, and endorsements. It is an honor to have all of them be a part of this book.

THE IMAGE ABOVE, WHICH I DREW WHEN I WAS A TEENAGER, WAS AN EARLY INDICATOR OF MY INTEREST IN UNDERSTANDING PAST AND PRESENT-DAY, AFRICAN-AMERICAN EXPERIENCES IN UNDER-RESOURCED CULTURES.

INTRODUCTION

It was during my first teaching experience that I started thinking about new ways to effectively manage students. Although I cared deeply about my students' learning, I focused mostly on trying to get them to behave.

The small, inner-city school where I taught was located in a blue-collar community west of Detroit and served just over 500 students, most of whom qualified for free lunch and/or breakfast programs and other federal resources. The community suffered economically with the collapse of the automotive industry and never regained the stability the industry once provided. The majority of the residents tried to support their families with minimum wage jobs. Those who could, left the city with their kids in tow and relocated to rural areas, leaving the inner-city schools with large populations of marginalized, under-resourced students.

My first year of teaching, I took over an elementary class in December for a teacher who had planned to retire in May but chose to leave early to avoid what she thought was an imminent mental breakdown. Other teachers, also overwhelmed with the challenges of teaching, were having breakdowns, taking leave, or quitting teaching altogether.

I was concerned that working in a classroom could jeopardize a teacher's mental health, but my concern paled in comparison to the excitement of having my first class. *How hard can this be?* I thought. *They're only children.*

DOSE OF REALITY

The class I took over was more challenging than I had anticipated. In fact, when submitting class size numbers to the state, I was allowed to count several of my students as two children because their behaviors were so taxing. What's more, my principal directed me to check one of my students each morning for a gun. The boy, Kashawn, was threatening to shoot the classroom aide and had described in graphic detail what the assault might look like.

Although Kashawn was only in elementary school, he was stout and already chest-high to me. He was no more loud or quiet than other students but at times would use his voice or quick, lurching forward movements to intimidate classmates, which he seemed to find humorous.

Looking for guidance, I discussed Kashawn's threats with the school social worker, who suggested I tape a small calendar to the corner of his desk. Each day that Kashawn didn't act out or threaten to shoot my aide, he would earn a sticker. At the end of the week, if he had accumulated five stickers, he would get a bag of M&Ms.

I understood her recommendation to use positive reinforcement to influence Kashawn's behavior, but something didn't seem quite right. Why should he get candy when the students who were behaving got nothing?

It was also during that first year of teaching that I learned never to order a student out of my classroom. Davonte had been acting out since the beginning of the term. He was active and boisterous and had a great deal of difficulty sitting still, being quiet, and keeping his hands to himself. There seemed to be a myriad of reasons for him to leave his seat and each time he did so he touched, poked, or hit a classmate or took something from their hands or desks.

One day, when Davonte had finally exhausted my patience, I ordered him out of the classroom to the principal's office. He refused, wrapped his legs around the legs of the chair, gripped the seat with both hands, and held on tightly. He looked at me with defiance as if to say, "What you gonna do now?" Not only was Davonte looking for my reaction, so were my 20-some other students.

The line in the sand had been drawn, and at that moment it seemed as if my entire reputation as a teacher hinged on getting him out of the classroom.

It took some doing, but I got Davonte to the office. I'm sure the way I handled it was against some kind of school district policy or state law, because the only way I could get him there was to drag him, still sitting in the chair, down the hall.

As it turned out, that first year of teaching wouldn't be the only time I would cross paths with Davonte. Years later when I was working as a college administrator, he visited my office looking for help registering for classes. As I worked with him, I couldn't help but wonder how I had contributed to the house arrest tether attached to his ankle. In that elementary classroom, had I unintentionally reinforced for Davonte the kind of relationship he would have with people in authority for many years to come? I might have won the battle the day I dragged him to the office, but in the end, I lost the war—and he was the casualty.

ATTAINING MY VISION

Some of the classroom management strategies I learned early on came from watching other teachers and seeking their advice. One teacher in my building punished students for misbehavior by making a spectacle of them, raising her voice, verbally shaming them, and marching them to stand in the corner. Others withheld snacks or kept disruptive students back from field trips or class parties. Often the students didn't make the connection between the punishment and their action, so rather than being remorseful and eager to change their behaviors, they were understandably confused and angry, which often led to more adverse behaviors.

Many teachers in my building had taught 20 years or more, and I thought they were the experts. I often followed suit when I didn't know what else to do, but I quickly understood the strategies they relied on seemed more about public classroom humiliation, punishment, and retaliation than about teaching students how to behave appropriately.

I soon came to realize that those approaches weren't for me. Maybe because I was already a parent when I began teaching, or maybe because of my own background in the public school system, I knew those strategies were ineffective at best, harmful at worst. Yet sometimes I followed suit when I didn't know what else to do.

I didn't want to *make* students behave. I wanted students to *want* to behave. I wanted to spend my time in the classroom teaching students, not managing their behaviors. Eventually I realized that I could not attain my vision of teaching and learning without first establishing a culture of reciprocal respect, willing cooperation, and predictable order.

It was then that I decided to focus on *my* behaviors. I committed to exploring my own thoughts, attitudes, and beliefs and how they impacted interactions with my students. My focus moved from responding to student behaviors to preventing opportunities for behaviors to get in the way of their success.

ON THE COLLEGE LEVEL

Although I continued working at the elementary school level, three years into my teaching career I took a position at a local community college as an adjunct instructor for developmental education reading classes. I was ready for something new and I thought my experience teaching young children to read would lend itself well to working with struggling college readers.

When I first began teaching at the college level, I believed that because college students had chosen to attend college, I would not encounter the kinds of behavior problems I'd encountered in K-12. I couldn't have been more wrong. I quickly learned that self-sabotaging behaviors follow first-generation, marginalized, underserved students from the K-12 system into the college classroom.

I do not in any way mean to imply that all—or only—first-generation, marginalized, underserved students are disruptive, struggling, or unengaged. Other students have difficulties, too. But I know that marginalized students, students who come from under-resourced areas, and first-generation students often lack the educational, social, emotional, and financial capital to successfully navigate the academic environment. The odds are against them. Historically, these students have been the most underprepared and least successful, often not persisting through their first year of college.

ROOTS OF DISCONNECT

Because of the current trend promoting college for all, never before have so many students had access to higher education. Some studies show that 36 percent of college freshmen are first-generation students. This is encouraging, however while the demographics of college students has shifted, college professors remain a fairly homogenous group. Nearly 80 percent of full-time college faculty and 77 percent of part-time faculty at degree-granting post-secondary institutions are white—and along with that, privileged.

Often disconnected from the experiences, beliefs, and attitudes of first-generation, marginalized students from underserved cultures, some faculty members—including faculty of color who are from more advantaged economic and cultural backgrounds than their students—struggle to effectively interact with various students and to create inclusive, equitable classroom environments where all students feel welcome and safe.

What is the root of this disconnect? Debby Irving, racial justice advocate, addresses this important issue in her book, *Waking Up White: And Finding Myself in the Story of Race*:

> I've often heard people debate the entangled relationship between race and class. "Which one is the real issue?" people ask. "Is it race or class?" I've

wondered myself how much of my socioeconomic advantage versus my skin color advantage shaped my life and skewed my worldview. I've come to believe it's not an either/or issue. Both are real, and both matter. Trying to determine which one is the "real" issue does a disservice to both. Concluding class is the real issue would give me permission to avoid thinking about race. Similarly, assuming race is the more significant issue overlooks the complications faced by white people caught in a vicious cycle of poverty. Both can trap people in a kind of second-class citizenship. If you can't get the education you need to get a job to pay for healthy food, medical care, transportation, and a home in a neighborhood with good schools, then you can't educate your children in a school that will prepare them for a job that will . . . and so on. Any cycle that traps someone in a state of perpetual advantage is the real issue for the person experiencing it. (13-14)

To be an effective teacher, I can't ignore that many of my students are from underserved cultures. I also can't ignore that nearly all of my students are African-American, first-generation students oftentimes with shared histories and cultures.

Student success or failure is frequently the product of what occurs in our classrooms—not only because financial aid is the lifeblood that allows students to remain registered in classes and students' financial aid is contingent upon grades and grades are generated in the classroom, but also because the classroom experience and interactions with faculty are often what drive students' feelings about higher education, their beliefs about their abilities to succeed, and their motivations to persist.

Because class time is a frequent driver of retention and persistence, it is crucial that faculty members understand the histories, experiences, beliefs, attitudes, and values of first-generation, marginalized students who come from under-resourced cultures.

As educators, we have to know our students and use that understanding as a foundation to teach, engage, motivate, encourage their success.

REFERENCE

Irving, Debby. *Waking Up White: And Finding Myself in the Story of Race.*
Elephant Room Press; 1 edition. 2014: 13-14.

CHAPTER 1
FLIPPING THE SCRIPT: REFRAMING PROBLEMS AND SOLUTIONS

Harvard Student Arrested In Class," a five-minute YouTube video of an in-class conflict between a college professor and her student, raised many questions in my mind about how teachers and students view each other and themselves. [You can view the video at www.youtube.com/watch?v=v2AmSMnAyeA.]

The incident was recorded on a cellphone in a college classroom; the camera remains on the student, although the instructor can be heard in the background. What begins as a heated verbal exchange between the student and instructor culminates in the violent removal of the student from class—in handcuffs—by three campus security officers.

Although we don't see what started the conflict, the dialogue between the instructor and the student suggests a clear disconnect, a marked lack of communication and understanding between the two. Yet, how did the situation get out of control so quickly? What prompted the instructor to summon security to have the student removed from class? Was the instructor afraid of the student? Did she have underlying beliefs or biases regarding the student? And, did the student have beliefs or biases about the instructor that drove her to such anger and frustration?

The instructor in the video seems to perceive the student as disruptive, obstinate, threatening, and combative. The student seems to believe her own behaviors and responses were justified and warranted and even states that the instructor was arguing with her and making her "get more uncomfortable and angry."

I'm certain the instructor believed she handled the situation professionally. Despite the student's loud and profane protests, the instructor remained calm and spoke with a steady voice. And I'm certain the student thought she, herself, handled the situation appropriately. Despite the instructor's arguments and ultimatums, the student remained seated and did not physically assault the instructor.

Despite arguing with the instructor, her use of profanity and refusal to leave the classroom, why would the student believe her own behavior was appropriate? Allow me to share a story that might help explain.

One afternoon, while I was walking Maya, my dog, to the cluster mailboxes in my neighborhood, an unleashed dog charged at us from a backyard. The dog was small but its aggressive charge and continuous high-pitched barking startled me. My faint-hearted 50-pound Golden Doodle recoiled.

I held still and began forcefully and repeatedly shouting, "No, no, no!" I hoped my loud shouts would stop the dog from advancing and alert the owner to get the unleashed dog under control. The owner soon appeared but he took no action other than to instruct the dog to "Get back to the house." The dog continued barking and advancing toward Maya and me.

I didn't want to run for fear the dog would chase us. Maya and I stood still. After a couple of minutes, the dog lost interest, turned around, and headed back to its house.

"I don't like it when your dog charges out," I told the owner, who was still standing in front of the house. "It scares me, and I don't want it to happen again."

He responded without apology, "I don't know how the dog got out. That dog is like Houdini," (despite the fact the dog was clearly unleashed and had come from the backyard).

I responded again firmly, "I do not like it when the dog charges me, and I don't want it to happen again."

Still no apology. "Ok," he finally said.

A couple of months later, the scenario repeated itself, except this time the dog was under the direction of the owner's wife who also made no attempt to physically restrain the dog. She only called it by name and shouted, "Get back to the house."

When the dog finally retreated, I said to her, "I've talked to your husband about this before. I do not like it when your dog charges me, and I want it to stop."

No apology. Instead she said, "I was putting the dog in the car, and she ran off."

"Leash her when you're taking her to the car and she won't be able to run off," I responded.

She said nothing but gave me a look as if to say, *Get over it.*

Several weeks later, Maya and I were assaulted at the mailbox again by the same dog. This time, as the owner's wife watched from the sidewalk, I slowly stepped back to retreat but the dog kept coming. Finally, as abruptly as the dog shot out, it withdrew and pranced back to the house.

The woman never attempted to restrain the dog nor did she speak to me.

Recounting the incident to my husband, I told him my patience had run its course and I was ready to act. In my anger I suggested several ways I could solve my problem, some of them outrageous and out of character. I asked which of my responses would embarrass him the least:

- Verbally and profanely berate the dog owners.
- Threaten to hurt the dog: "Either you stop the dog from charging out or I will."
- Carry a can of mace and threaten to use it.

Of course, I would never hurt the dog, however, in my anger those thoughts came to mind. My husband thought for a minute and said, "I will support any of those ideas and none of them will embarrass me."

His response took the wind out of my sails. He did not oppose me, tell me the options I presented were extreme, or point out the zero chance I would carry out any of the ideas. He just let me vent.

Later that evening as we were driving through an area of town known for poverty, violence, and gunfire, I noticed a man walking on the sidewalk with his leashed dog. I wondered how that man would respond if a dog came charging at them. The man might react in a volatile way, as I had talked about doing. He may feel disrespected and feel the need to respond to that disrespect. He may not know any other way to respond than to fight back.

I understood the anger and frustration of being disrespected; the dog owners who let their animal charge at me clearly disregarded my feelings, rights, and safety. If all I had was my respect (and my dog) and if I didn't have much to lose, it's likely I would have responded in a very different way. I might have acted not only to protect my dog and me from physical harm but also to assert my right to be respected. If I didn't respond I might appear weak or scared, which would make me a target in my surroundings.

UNDERSTANDING BEHAVIOR

So, getting back to the student in the YouTube video, is it possible that first-generation, marginalized students sometimes feel as vulnerable and disrespected in the classroom environment as I felt being threatened by the dog? Do they feel pressured to assert themselves to maintain their respect because sometimes that's all they have? Are they actually masking fear with anger, aggression, or apathy?

If their lack of experience in a higher education environment makes them feel vulnerable or classroom interactions threaten their sense of self, students likely will hold on even tighter to the responses they've used their entire lives to protect themselves. Those responses are sometimes as outrageous and counterproductive as the actions I concocted in response to the dog incident.

I am an educated, professional woman with resources at my access and a host of acceptable strategies to deal with unpleasant situations. Yet in a moment of disrespect and fear I, too, contemplated using whatever means were necessary to get what I needed: to feel safe and respected.

A yawning gap exists between how instructors perceive the classroom behaviors of first-generation, marginalized students from under-resourced cultures and how the students themselves perceive the same behaviors. For example, when I ask instructors to identify disengaged or disruptive student behaviors they've observed in the classroom, these are some of their responses:

- Arriving late to class
- Repeated absences
- Using phones during class (texting, Facebooking, Tweeting, etc.)
- Wearing ear buds
- Cheating
- Sleeping
- Talking when the instructor or classmates are talking
- Not participating or engaging
- Coming to class high
- Bringing children to class
- Not bringing course materials to class
- Repeatedly going in and out of the classroom
- Impulsively commenting on the instructor's lecture
- Monopolizing class or group discussions
- Making disrespectful, inappropriate, aggressive, or threatening comments to the instructor or classmates

- Confronting or arguing with the instructor or classmates
- Fighting

These behaviors have brought about life-altering consequences, including failing grades, loss of financial aid, loss of credits toward graduation, dismissal from athletic teams, loss of campus housing, suspension or expulsion, and in some cases arrests and incarceration. So, given these unfavorable consequences, how do students rationalize these actions?

CORNERSTONES OF DENIAL

Many students have been exhibiting unproductive behaviors since grade school, enduring the negative consequences, and sabotaging their own success. Why do they keep returning to those behaviors? Here are four cornerstones of denial that explain students' unproductive yet repeated behaviors:

Minimize—downplay the behavior or the effects.
- "I wasn't talking that loud."
- "I was only 20 minutes late and the instructor flipped out."
- "I only missed 12 days of class."

Justify—make excuses for the behavior to cast it in a different light.
- "I only cheated because I need to keep my place on the team."
- "I only cussed at the professor when I felt disrespected."
- "Other people are cheating, too, and the professor grades on a curve, so I had to cheat."

Blame—point the finger at others.
- "This girl keeps talking shit about me so I had to make her shut her mouth."
- "The professor is a jerk and doesn't like me. He kicked me out of his class."

Rationalize—attempt to bring reason to otherwise unworkable actions.

- "I studied two hours last night. I put my time in. I don't need to listen right now."
- "I didn't get any sleep last night. It's not hurting anybody in this class if I'm sleeping."
- "If I come to class high, I'm able to focus more."

The cornerstones of denial and the stories students often tell themselves to rationalize continuing behaviors is only part of the story. We must also explore what drives students' behaviors.

CONSIDERING CONTEXT

Instructors interpret or explain students' unproductive and disruptive behaviors in many ways, including the following:

- Students don't care about their education—they're only in college to collect financial aid money.
- Students don't like/respect their instructor.
- Students are lazy.
- Students are rude.
- Students aren't college material.

We must take a closer look at what drives student behavior to understand that behavior. For example, what might cause a student to be absent? Could repeated absences stem from a *fear* of failing? What might prompt a student to carry a weapon? Could *fear* for their safety prompt that type of behavior? Or maybe it's a need for power?

Changing perspectives and considering the underlying reasons for disruptive behaviors is similar to looking at one of those dual black-and-white drawings that displays a different image depending on whether you're looking at the white or the black parts as background or foreground.

The disruptive classroom behaviors that instructors see as *problems* might actually be students' *solutions* to their problems. A student who is feeling afraid or powerless might decide carrying a weapon is the solution. A student who is afraid of failing might stop paying attention and talk to his classmate instead—after all, it's better to be thought of as a slacker than as stupid.

It follows, then, that when professors address the behaviors as problems, they are threatening the students' coping strategies.

Let's go back to the instructor in the YouTube video. The professor leveraged her authority as the instructor, ordered the student out of class, and called security because her actions were driven by her thoughts and beliefs. We don't know the specifics on the circumstances, but she might have thought the student was trying to bully another student. She might have thought the student was dangerous. She might have thought the student was a troublemaker. However, if she considered the root of the student's behaviors, she might have engaged with the student in a different way that would have changed the outcome.

Of course, these students are not going to tell us where these self-sabotaging behaviors are coming from. Most don't know themselves, but even the ones who do know aren't going to make themselves vulnerable enough to say, "Look, here's the thing, I don't have the best reading, writing, and math skills. Nobody in my family went to college before me. I'm scared of looking stupid. I feel like I'm missing something the other students seem to have, and I feel like I don't belong here. If I have to act tough, uninterested, and sometimes even disrespectful, then I will. If I have to come late, come high, come carrying a pistol, or not come at all so I don't feel alone or afraid or powerless, that's what I'm going to do. And, if I fail, lose my financial aid, or get kicked out, it's still better than feeling insecure, ashamed, and afraid."

Remember, our thoughts, beliefs, and interpretations about our students' behaviors drive our responses. They often dictate how we engage and respond to our students. Understanding their lives and their struggles gives us the opportunity to ultimately break the cycle of negative behavior and increase engagement, cooperation, and success.

I don't propose that professors ignore or tolerate negative student behaviors. I simply argue that we must view them in a different context and engage students in an empathic way that produces trust, mutual respect, and collaboration. Professors who understand what negative behaviors represent in a student's life can build the type of rapport that promotes student success and campus equity.

STUDENTS WITH GRIT

Psychologist Angela Duckworth (2016) contends that having grit—a passion and perseverance for very long-term goals—is an essential component of success independent of and beyond what talent and intelligence contribute. Some believe that college students, especially first-generation college students, lack grit, focus, determination, tenacity, and resiliency, perhaps because they are ill-prepared or lazy. I would argue, though, that first-generation students demonstrate exorbitant grit, especially first-generation, marginalized students from under-resourced cultures.

They often have endured significant challenges, including loss of family members to divorce, violence, alcohol, drugs, incarceration, or death. Some live or have lived in low-income or poverty situations, and some have been homeless. Some students have moved residences and school districts more times during their K-12 years than most people do in a lifetime. Others have been victims of physical, emotional, or sexual abuse, and some have been victims of violence, racism, or bullying.

Yet these tenacious students still have the grit and resilience to apply to colleges, navigate financial aid forms, visit campuses, register for courses, attend orientations, acquire class materials, locate resources, be in environments that often do not welcome or celebrate them, and against all odds, go to class.

Imagine the strength it takes to deal with the challenges of not feeling safe, of having inadequate supports, and lacking economic resources. What would be seemingly inconsequential challenges for many are major obstacles to their success.

For example, for students who are not economically disadvantaged, getting a flat tire on the way to school with no spare would likely be a mere inconvenience. They call a tow service to bring them a tire or tow their car to a tire service center. They might be late for school, but they would be on their way.

The same situation for those who are struggling economically presents an entirely different scenario. Without money for a tow truck or a tire, they would have to begin networking to find a ride to school. They might try to borrow money from a friend or family member to buy a tire or look for something to trade in exchange for money, such as a bike, food card, or cellphone.

Then there's the challenge of actually getting someplace to buy a tire and then putting it on the car. Likely they would need to purchase the cheapest new or used tire available, making it likely the same scenario would soon repeat itself.

They would be late to school, just like the more advantaged student, but the playing field doesn't level there. This likely would be just one of many times an economic roadblock prevented them from arriving to school or work on time, so they might risk failing the class or losing their job.

What might be perceived as students' lack of grit might be less about perseverance and more about equity and students' skepticism about the payoff for the challenges they'll endure and the sacrifices they'll have to make to achieve a college education.

The idea of struggling with food, housing, and transportation insecurities in addition to the loneliness of being away from family and the stress of feeling like an ill-prepared outsider for two, four, or even six years for an undergraduate degree can leave even the most hopeful student feeling like the sacrifices are too high for uncertain outcomes that are often laced with insurmountable student loan debt.

Even if students believe the payoff is worth the struggle, the reward often seems too far down the road to be within reach.

Students have grit. What they need are equitable opportunities. Our job is to make sure students have those opportunities and to teach them how to apply their well-developed sense of perseverance and resiliency to a setting where the culture, expectations, and requirements are unfamiliar.

Instructors can assist students in applying their grit and skills of perseverance to their new environment on college campuses by first providing classroom and campus spaces where students feel comfortable and supported. When students feel welcome and safe knowing instructors have their best interest in mind, they are more likely to become receptive to the instruction and guidance that will teach them how to transfer their strength and resiliency to the academic environment. For example, instructors can point out that students already have what it takes to make it to graduation: persistence, resiliency, strength, and commitment.

Most important, what first-generation, marginalized students from under-resourced cultures have is an ability to adapt to challenging situations. They can take that strength and use it to adjust to the demands of higher education.

WHAT WE CAN DO

Educators sometimes struggle to understand why students have such difficulty making changes when they want to be successful and they know the negative outcomes of self-sabotaging behaviors. We want to provide alternate behavior solutions for our students so their previous, undesirable behaviors fall away on their own.

Consider the Five Stages of Change that were developed by Drs. James Prochaska and Carlo DiClemente in the late 1970s as a way to understand the process of change students are likely to experience as they navigate higher education.

1. **Pre-contemplation:** Students are often unaware there is a problem and aren't thinking about change. They continue to rely on previous responses and behaviors to navigate the demands of higher education.

2. **Contemplation:** Students are beginning to suspect there is a problem (previous behaviors aren't bringing the results they desire) but they aren't yet ready to make a change.

3. **Preparation:** Students are aware there is a problem and are preparing to take action. This might include thinking about things successful students have done, thinking about ways to make the change such as making an appointment to meet with a tutor, getting materials ready before class, etc.

4. **Action:** Students are ready and actually move forward to make the change. This might include meeting with an advisor or tutor, meeting with a study group, etc.

5. **Maintenance:** Students are continuing with the change they've made and work to keep the change active.

Change is fluid, and it is likely students will fluctuate between contemplation, preparation, and action. Before responding to students who exhibit self-sabotaging behaviors that impede their success, it's helpful for faculty to know where students are in the stage of change. Professors who jump in too quickly with intervention strategies that are more appropriate for behaviors further along in the change process can inadvertently distance students and prompt them to discount or ignore the professor.

Because many first-generation students are in the pre-contemplative or contemplative stage of change, a more effective approach might be to ask questions that encourage students' curiosity about what has prompted their behaviors and inquire about their feelings about their outcomes. For example, "I notice you are spending a lot of time on your phone. In the past, what outcomes have resulted from time spent on your phone in class?"

Professors, too, are likely to experience the Five Stages of Change as they explore their thoughts, attitudes, biases, and beliefs and consider utilizing an empathic, compassionate approach with first-generation, marginalized students from under-resourced cultures.

Here's how the Five Stages of Change might look for faculty members:

1. **Pre-contemplation:** Faculty are often unaware there is a problem and aren't thinking about change. They continue to rely on previous responses, strategies, and behaviors when engaging with students.

2. **Contemplation:** Faculty are beginning to suspect there is a problem (previous responses, strategies, and behaviors aren't bringing the student results they desire), but they aren't yet ready to make a change.

3. **Preparation:** Faculty are aware there is a problem and are preparing to take action. That might include reflecting on their cultural or racial biases, thinking about things other faculty have done that resulted in high retention and student success rates, thinking about ways to make changes such as registering for professional development opportunities, thinking about reviewing retention strategies, etc.

4. **Action:** Faculty are now ready and actually move forward to make the change. This might include actively exploring their thoughts, attitudes, biases, and beliefs using a cognitive behavioral therapy approach, applying rapport and retention strategies, actively considering the root of students' self-sabotaging behaviors before responding, etc.

5. **Maintenance:** Faculty are continuing with the change they've made and work to keep the change active.

Like students, faculty members are likely to fluctuate between contemplation, preparation, and action. When faculty know where they are in terms of their own stages of change, it allows them to explore the reasons they might be resistant to change.

For example, faculty may be resistant to change due to their racial or cultural biases or prejudices. As faculty, reflecting on our thoughts, attitudes, and beliefs that we may secretly or publicly have about our students will position us to become better aware of what is influencing our teaching and will also provide opportunities for us to become better resources to our students. When changing our thoughts, etc. to be culturally sensitive in our classrooms, we may initially become overly critical of self once we have reflected on the culturally bias messages learned through our own childhood. We may also begin to feel a sense of helplessness or motivation after we have identified the need for change in how we think about our students that influence how we behave toward our students. However, similarly to the Five Stages of Change, Helms (1990) Racial Identity Inventory located in, *Black and White Racial Identity: Theory, Research, and Practice* shared how we can locate our cultural attitudes amongst the following six-stage model. Each stage identifies where a person may be in his or her own cultural awareness and appropriateness based on the thought and belief.

Dr. LaShonda Fuller, a Faculty Specialist from Western Michigan University, notes in the excerpt below, the similarity of the Five Stages of Change to Helms (1990) Racial Identity Inventory located in, Black and White Racial Identity: Theory, Research, and Practice. The stages provide an opportunity for people, in this case instructors, to identify where they may be in his or her own cultural awareness and appropriateness based on their thoughts and beliefs. Fuller describes each of Helms' stages to help instructors identify their cultural awareness.

Contact—All people should be treated equally. There is no acknowledgment of race and ethnicity. Persons in the Contact stage from the dominant culture maintain a surface level contact of interaction with people from other races and an attitude that dismisses any influence of race and ethnicity. The Contact stage can potentially be offensive to others and discount what racially different individuals may have had to endure throughout history that individuals from the dominant culture have not had to experience. An example of an inappropriate statement that represents the Contact stage is, "I don't see race."

Disintegration—Some awareness of cultural differences develops. May attribute these differences to intrapsychic or contextual variables such as poverty. This stage gives reverence to a group of people's experience, which has had influence on how this group of people within a larger culture views the world. This stage represents the experience people from the dominant culture has when they begin to acknowledge how the world views one person over another person within the larger culture. For example, a person from the dominant culture acknowledges that within the American culture, Black men are racially profiled by police officers more often than White men due to racially stereotypical views of Black men seen as criminals. This stage still represents a surface level knowledge and acceptance of cultural differences from one's own racial group. This stage still represents a surface level knowledge *and* **acceptance** of cultural differences from one's own racial group.

Reintegration—Awareness of differences; culturally different seen as inferior. When a person of the dominant race and culture seeks to reintegrate, Helms (1990) model implies that the person from the dominant culture has conducted more research on underserved cultures and has accepted the reality that inferiority exists within the larger operating systems that serve all people.

Pseudo-Independent—The belief that the culturally different group should adopt the values of the dominant group. The dominant group has a genuine desire to assist with the value adoption. Once a person of the dominant race becomes aware of other races and cultures, there is a possibility that the individual secretly or publicly believes that if people from other cultures align themselves (acculturate) with "my culture" (the dominant culture) situations will be different for the underserved populations.

Immersion/Emersion—Wants to learn more about other cultures and engages in activities that will improve knowledge and skill base. This stage of the cultural identity development model is action oriented. Here, a person from the dominant culture immerses themselves within underserved cultures to gain a compassionate understanding of other's life experiences. Action may also look like continually working toward better cultural competency in order to honor, represent, and empower all student populations.

Autonomous—Values cultural difference and consistently uses culturally appropriate strategies. Understands that injustices have occurred and may work to correct these injustices. The final stage indicates an appreciation of self and others by illustrating respect for cultural differences. Ultimately, the expectation of this stage is for one to become culturally aware and understand that our purpose includes changing systems that perpetuate inferiority, racism, and hate. As faculty, we can be respectful and welcoming when engaging with those from cultures different from our own; be inclusive when teaching by including and addressing cultural influences and nuances; and connecting with those from different cultures to expand our own cultural experiences and awareness.

UNDERSTANDING THE STUDENT EXPERIENCE: MARTEL'S STORY

PERSEVERANCE IN THE FACE OF PAIN

Whenever I think of grit I think of Martel. Martel was a student in my college class that was largely made up of young men from inner-city Detroit. The students seemed to come together as a group, but, as is often the case with young men, especially young men from under-resourced cultures, there can be tendencies to guard their feelings so they don't appear weak or vulnerable.

On the day of student presentations, during the last week of the term, the lights were dim and the projector beamed the first slide of Martel's PowerPoint on the screen. He took his place at the front of the class and introduced his topic: gun violence.

"This next slide provides a definition of gun violence," Martel announced. He continued, "This third slide shows a picture of my high school. I chose this topic because my cousin . . ."

Martel dropped his head and put his hand over his face. The room fell silent as he struggled to hold back his tears.

My first instinct was to rush over to him, to treat him like I would one of my own sons. The mother in me wanted to pick up his 6-foot-2-inch, 250-pound body, tell him everything was going to be OK, and carry him away to safety.

I knew I couldn't. I had to let him work through it in his own way. Quietly, I said, "Take your time, Martel," and then I waited in silence with the class.

It was only seconds, but seemed like minutes, before Martel walked out of the classroom.

Nobody moved. Nobody spoke. I kept my eyes on the PowerPoint slide that was still projected on the screen. The students, too, waited in silence. A couple of minutes later, Martel re-entered the room and took his place at the front of the class. "I'm sorry," he said quietly.

"No worries," I said. "Begin when you're ready."

When he finished the presentation, Martel said, "My cousin was killed by gun violence. I was just telling him that day that he had to get out of that stuff. We'd always take the bus together but there was a pep rally that day so I stayed after school but he went on. Someone sprayed the bus stop with bullets, and he was shot and killed. We were close."

"I'm so sorry, Martel," I said softly. "It sounds like you, too, might have been a victim if you'd left with him that day."

He nodded his head, picked up his book bag, and left for the day.

We sat quietly.

Moments later, Keon volunteered to present his slides. He projected his first slide on the screen, but before beginning he made a forceful statement, emphasizing each word as if we would all understand it better if he said it with deliberation, "Martel's school was no joke."

I looked at Keon, nodded my head, and said, "I get it."

Then, he started his presentation.

Keon and Martel weren't really friends, but it was important to Keon that everyone in the room who saw Martel cry understood clearly how rough the school was—painfully rough. It was as if Keon were saying, "If you only knew what it was like, you'd be crying, too. So, don't judge him." I know Martel had grit, as evidenced by the fact that against all odds, he was still breathing, pressing on, coming to class, and believing things could be better.

Watching him struggle was one of the hardest moments I have had in higher education. It's hard to watch anybody cry, but there's something especially heart-wrenching about seeing a young man cry when you know how fiercely he wants to protect himself from being seen as weak or vulnerable.

REFERENCES

Duckworth, A. *Grit: The Power of Passion and Perseverance.* New York: Scribner. https://www.newharbinger.com/blog/what-grit-and-why-it-important. 2016.

Helms, J. E. *Black and white racial identity: Theory, research, and practice.* Westport, CT: Greenwood Publishing Group, Inc. 1990.

In Norcross, John C. and Goldfried, Marvin R. *Handbook of Psychotherapy Integration.* Oxford series in clinical psychology (2nd ed.). New York: Oxford University Press. 2005.

CHAPTER 2
RECOGNIZING PERCEPTIONS, BIASES, AND DISENGAGEMENT

To engage with students in ways that build rapport, encourage cooperation, and promote success, instructors must be aware of students' beliefs and experiences and ensure all students feel acknowledged and supported.

Those educators who teach *content* rather than *students* might argue that it's not the instructor's responsibility to understand the history or attitudes of their students. "I teach math," they say, "It's not my job to learn about students' personal lives."

However, education is a human services profession, and educators should be committed to the learning and advancement of students. It makes sense, then, to consider students' K-12 experiences, the cultures of their neighborhoods and families, their experiences with authority figures, the strategies they have developed to solve their problems—all the things that factor into students' behavior, engagement, performance, and success.

THE RIFT THAT SEPARATES

When *Elysian Dreams* author B. J. Neblett said, "We are the sum total of our experiences. Those experiences—be they positive or negative—make us the person we are, at any given point in our lives," he wasn't talking specifically about college students, but his observation shines light on the fact that students' beliefs and experiences follow them into the classroom. A white faculty member mentioned some of her first-generation black students seemed to walk into class on the first day of the semester with a contentious attitude toward her. She was baffled.

"They don't even know me. How can they already have an attitude with me?" she wondered.

Because of past negative racial experiences both in and out of school, some first-generation, marginalized students who come from under-resourced cultures have developed an aversion to authority figures. College professors are authority figures, as are college administrators and staff, human services workers, social workers, security officers, police officers, probation officers, and judges.

Because professors are authority figures, students sometimes view them with distrust and contempt, seeing them as adversaries before getting to know them. Influenced by negative experiences of racism, discrimination, oppression, and powerlessness within society and educational systems, students' communication with instructors and campus staff is often guarded, untrusting, and self-protective, which in and of itself hampers any kind of positive relationship between student and instructor.

My students routinely share the everyday occurrences of discrimination and prejudice they encounter. One such student, Tirey, wrote a post on Facebook about an experience he had in a drugstore parking lot.

Tirey was leaving the store when an older Caucasian woman who was entering the store suddenly stopped, looked at him, and went back to her car to lock the doors before proceeding into the building.

The fact that Tirey wrote the post demonstrated his strong feelings about the incident and as he made clear in his own youthful vernacular, he had no intention of stealing anything from her car.

Whether Tirey accurately interpreted the woman's actions is not as important as how her behavior made him feel; almost instantly he was psychologically transformed from a bright college student to a menacing thief. Although he publicly defended himself through social media, he had internalized the incident and carried it with him, adding it to the host of other experiences that have perpetuated his beliefs about himself.

PERCEPTIONS OF SELF

Black historian, sociologist, and civil rights activist W.E.B. Du Bois first explored the concept of two different and distinct perceptions of self in his 1903 publication *The Souls of Black Folk*. Du Bois coined the term *double consciousness* to describe the internal conflict of African-American people who simultaneously see their selves through their own eyes and from the point of view of contemptuous others (White America).

African-American males, for example, carry the burden of knowing how they are viewed by society, which is in conflict with what they believe about themselves. Simultaneously, they want to uphold the ideals of the country in which they reside. In their families, neighborhoods, and churches, their perceptions of themselves stand in opposition to how they are often perceived by society. This conflict is carried through the classroom door in both the K-12 system and higher education.

It would be nearly impossible for first-generation, underserved students to endure such experiences and come away feeling anything other than uncertainty and self-doubt about their ability to belong and succeed in higher education as well as suspicion about the sincerity and trustworthiness of those in authority who are there to help and support their success. How could it be any different for marginalized students? Aren't they, too, the sum of their experiences and the experiences of their families?

The sum experience of marginalized students understandably includes their own experiences, the experiences of generations of family members, and the experiences of people they will never meet but know through historical accounts, news coverage, or social media: Emmett Till, Trayvon Martin, James Brown, Eric Garner, Sandra Bland, and too many others to name.

This certainly might explain why marginalized students may have what my colleague called a "contentious attitude" on the first day of the semester. Students, especially black male students, may have a preconceived notion that professors have unfavorable, stereotypical opinions about them and thus avoid engaging with professors or going to them for help. Dr. Luke Wood, a San Diego University education professor whose research focuses on "factors affecting the success of boys and men of color in education," states, "Black male students are less inclined to approach faculty, fearing that they will be seen as underprepared for college-level work, destined for failure in college, and unwelcome in the campus community. Unfortunately, much of this fear is rooted in stereotypical perceptions of Black men in society as being unintelligent and indolent" (Wood, 2014).

People of common backgrounds or ideologies form groups—families, tribes, and communities—that sometimes adopt the idea, "If you're not one of us, you must be against us." If professors want first-generation, marginalized students from under-resourced cultures to be successful, they must work deliberately and purposely to understand students' beliefs and experiences and develop a rapport with them to convey they are all a part of the same group: the classroom group. Professors should intentionally let students know they are on their side *and earn* students' trust if they want their students to be open, engaged, and receptive to learning in the classroom.

A communications professor from a nearby college shared a story about a conversation he'd had with a first generation, marginalized student who was homeless about the importance of saving money. When the professor talked with the student about long-term financial planning, he disconnected himself from the student. Instead of the student coming away from the conversation with a financial plan, I suspect he came away with nothing more than validation that the professor didn't understand his circumstances—a crucial aspect of relationship building.

Intentionally being careful not to offend students will not close the distance either. There needs to be intentional effort to forge relationships, develop trust, and become a part of the students' group. On his blog, Straight Talk, social marketing strategist Ted Rubin discusses the importance of leaders connecting with those they hope to influence, and his advice applies to college professors, too, "Indifference is expensive. Hostility is unaffordable. Trust is priceless. It's all about relationships."

What about professors who say, "I treat all my students the same"? They might believe that is a fair approach, but it isn't. We can't treat all students the same because they are not all the same. Students have different experiences, histories, cultures, values, and beliefs.

Professors who were not first-generation, marginalized students from under-resourced cultures can gain insider knowledge about the beliefs, attitudes, and experiences of their students by observing, listening to, engaging with, and getting to know their students and becoming aware of their students' cultures and histories. Faculty can participate in professional development opportunities that promote understanding and provide strategies for relationship building.

Instructors who make it their business to be interested in and learn about their students will project care and compassion; their students will respond with trust, respect, and engagement.

STUDENTS ARE NOT THE ONLY ONES

Like students, professors too, carry their experiences and the experiences of their families and loved ones into the classroom with them, allowing them to build schema that influence how they interact with the world until new information is revealed. Professors might attach racially stereotyped behaviors and characteristics to their students, such as assuming they know students' programs of study, athletic abilities, work ethic, and even music preferences. For example, some professors might assume all black students like rap/hip-hop music. In addition, the stereotypes of black people as dangerous, volatile criminals as depicted in the media and entertainment likely cause some professors to avoid engaging with black students, particularly black male students.

My own early experiences, the experiences of my family, and even the information I took in from the media contributed to my early beliefs about black culture people. My family's beliefs were wildly inaccurate, but they influenced my view of the racial world as I listened to them refer to black people as loud, violent, knife-wielding thugs who always fought in groups.

I am sure that contributed to my reaction to one of my earliest interactions with black people when I was five. My mother left my brother and me in the car while she ran into a store. The store was in a predominately black, urban neighborhood. Within minutes of my mother entering the store, a small group of middle school black boys approached our car. My brother said, "I know these guys from school."

Although there was nothing alarming about what he said or the way he said it, as I watched my brother lean over and lock the car doors, I knew the boys weren't my brother's friends. They began pounding on the windows saying they were going to pull my brother out of the car and "beat his ass." I was terrified.

I don't remember how the situation ended—whether they left on their own, they saw my mother coming out of the store, or someone intervened. I was far too young to understand that one experience wasn't representative of the behaviors of an entire population. That experience reinforced the idea that my family's beliefs were valid and accurate and became a part of my sum total of experiences. I formed a judgment about black youth that I only later came to understand was inaccurate.

Faculty who have limited experience with marginalized populations or under-resourced cultures might be uncomfortable or even fearful about engaging with students from these groups. Based on his research, Luke Wood (2014) concluded that because of educators' apprehension about engaging, combined with the "approach me first" and "prove yourself first" stances, many faculty members and black men never meaningfully engage with one another."

First-generation, marginalized students who come from under-resourced cultures are heavily influenced by and dependent on relationships with others, as relationships are sometimes all they have. The people in their lives often mean more to them than material possessions or some far-off impalpable college degree.

At times I've heard professors offhandedly say they do not care if students like them. They might have added that their goal is not to be *liked* by students but to *teach* students. Instructors who feel this way might not understand if there is no relationship, there is no learning. When students sincerely believe their instructor cares about them, respects them, and wants them to be successful, they are more likely to engage, cooperate, and find success.

UNDERSTANDING THE STUDENT EXPERIENCE: JAYVON'S STORY

LOOKING FOR THE POSITIVE

Jayvon displayed an attitude starting the first day of class. It could be seen in the way he walked, the way he talked, and even in the way he moved. I imagined the other students wanted to steer clear of him to avoid any type of potential confrontation. It appeared an accidental bump or an inadvertent look might prompt an unpleasant if not explosive reaction from him.

A few weeks into the semester, while the class was reading a passage from a novel, we came upon a section that described the father as being irresponsible and detached from his children.

Unexpectedly and spontaneously Jayvon angrily announced, with his facial expression and body language doing most of the talking, "I don't want my dad's last name!"

He was visibly angry and the class, not knowing what to do, became still and quiet.

"It sounds like you're pretty angry," I said.

"I am. He cheated on my mama and left when I was two." Then he added, "My mama put a whoopin' on her, though."

I decided to ignore the "whoopin'" comment and focus on Jayvon.

"It sounds like you haven't seen your dad in a long time."

"That's right. And, now he's coming around and wants to see me. I don't want to see him! I don't even want his name!"

"Well, let me see," I said in a matter of fact tone. "If your dad left when you were two and you're eighteen now," I looked up at the ceiling like I was thinking, "that means he's been gone, and you've been angry, for about the past sixteen years, right?"

"Yup," he responded.

"Alright. Well, how much longer do you plan on being angry? How much longer are you going to carry that anger around with you? Five more years? Ten more? Sixteen?" I asked.

Jayvon stared at me blankly as the students continued to look on in silence.

Finally, in a much quieter tone he said, "My mama says being angry doesn't hurt him. It only hurts me."

"Your mom is a smart woman. Seems like it might be time to let it go, Jayvon."

It was then that he so simply and honestly admitted, "I don't know how."

From the beginning of the semester, I found it difficult to like Jayvon. I might have even silently hoped he'd drop the class. I couldn't see how I was going to bring this group of students together with a sense of community if they were intimidated by or scared of Jayvon.

When this incident happened, I thought about what was driving his behavior: He was hurting. He had to throw his weight around to feel important and worthy. When he didn't get what he needed from his dad, he found a solution to his problem to get what he needed in other ways.

That day changed the way I interacted with Jayvon. This is how he started his end-of-term letter, "I have really liked being in this class, you make me feel at home." And this is how the letter ended, "Miss Amelia will never let you quit and care about you like you were her own child."

REFERENCE

Wood, JL. Apprehension to engagement in the classroom: Perceptions of black males in the community college. *International Journal of Qualitative Studies in Education.* 2014:27(6), 785-803.

CHAPTER 3
NAVIGATING BELIEFS, EXPERIENCES, AND BEHAVIORS OF UNDER-RESOURCED CULTURES

If instructors want students to learn and be successful, they must get students on their side by being on the students' side. If instructors want their students to attend class, complete assignments, engage, and succeed in their classes, they must focus on developing rapport with students by understanding who they are—their beliefs, experiences, and behaviors.

Dr. Ruby K. Payne, author of A *Framework for Understanding Poverty*, teaches on the mindsets of economic classes and overcoming the hurdles of poverty. I've seen firsthand how some of these mindsets and behaviors of poverty play out—in specific regard to first-generation, marginalized students—in the college classroom. The information in this chapter builds, in part, on Payne's ideas, first introduced in 1995, and is adapted and expanded by my own theoretical research and observation. What I have found is that it is essential that college instructors understand the "hidden rules" of the poverty mindset and critical role they play in their students' success in education.

SELF-ESTEEM AND DEFICITS

Despite efforts to level the playing field with early education childhood programs, underserved students continue to arrive at school with deficits, and those deficits follow them throughout their schooling. Students know early on who has free or reduced-price lunch, who rides the bus from the least desirable neighborhoods, who does not wear trendy clothes, and who is in lower reading groups.

Deficits breed unproductive behaviors, which lead to tensions with educators, which cause negative feelings toward students, which lead to resistance from students, which cause more unproductive behaviors, and so on. By the time students get to college, they often have had a lifetime of negative educational experiences that have left them feeling like marginalized outsiders.

Two such students sat in the back row of my class. Jamal and Amere both came from one of the most under-resourced areas in Detroit. Both were on academic probation due to their lack of success the previous semester and were required to show proof that they attended the Student Success Center for one-on-one tutoring if they wanted to continue living in campus housing.

A few times after class, I asked if they had been to the center and received vague answers about their intentions of going. One afternoon, I decided they needed a more interceptive approach. After dismissing class a few minutes early, I asked if they would walk with me to the center. They agreed.

When we arrived at the center, I showed them how to check in using the electronic system and introduced them to faculty tutors. I invited them to stay and work on their assignments and reminded them they needed to comply with their academic probation requirements. They agreed to stay, and I told them I would come back and check on them in a little while.

When I checked back 30 minutes later, Amere was working through some math problems with a tutor while Jamal was intently engaged with two of his phones.

I pulled up a chair. "How can I help you get started?" I asked.

"I dunno," he said with eyes still on his phones.

"You have a writing class this semester, and I think your next assignment is a personal essay, correct?"

"Yeah."

"Let's see what you have so far."

Jamal pulled out a notebook where he had written some notes about a day his house was robbed. We worked together on his paper for a while, and I left feeling optimistic about the progress both young men had made.

I realized that taking the students to the center instead of suggesting they go was the key. The center was new to them, and they likely weren't comfortable with the unfamiliar check-in system. I also thought about the importance of working alongside students. Students, especially first-generation students, need to have someone support them so they don't feel like they are alone. They need someone to help them get started and encourage them to continue when they feel like giving up.

Later in the semester, a class activity shed further light on Jamal and his self-image.

I sometimes conduct the Affirmation Whisper Activity from Skip Downing's *On Course* workshop (http://oncourseworkshop. com/?s=whisper+affirmations) to help students learn to alter negative self-perceptions and self-talk as they move forward in their journeys. I use it only with groups that have developed unusually strong bonds among their classmates and with me.

Students first create a statement about themselves regarding three of their own best qualities. For example: "I am a bright, athletic, and kind woman," or "I am a loyal, smart, and honest man." Then half of the students sit in randomly placed chairs in the center of a cleared classroom, with eyes closed, lights dimmed, and soft music playing. The other half of the students walk quietly from seated classmate to seated classmate and whisper a variation of their own statement in their classmates' ear, changing the "I" to "You." The statements become, for example: "*You* are a bright, athletic, and kind woman," or "*You* are a loyal, smart, and honest man."

The students continue to move around the room for several minutes, sometimes going to the same person more than once. After several minutes, the seated students switch places with the whispering students and the process repeats. Even though the students whisper their own personal statements to others, it is a moving experience for the seated students who are enveloped with kind, uplifting statements from their classmates.

In the last week of Jamal and Amere's class, I asked the students to write the statements about themselves and then explained how we would use them. I emphasized the need for seriousness and suggested students leave the room and wait in the hall until the activity was over if they were prone to giggling or had a hard time being quiet, as it would detract from the experience. All the students chose to stay for the activity.

I watched carefully as the students whispered in the ears of their classmates, but I paid special attention to Jamal and Amere moving about the room, completely engaged in the process. When students switched places and the activity continued, Amere and Jamal were seated quietly with eyes closed, listening intently to the whispered messages.

I participated as well, but my whispers were not stock statements prepared about myself. My whispers were personal statements developed spontaneously for each individual student. When I got to Jamal, I whispered, "Jamal, you are a bright, strong young man, and you *are* going to be very successful."

When the activity concluded, I brightened the classroom lights and asked the students to discuss how they felt about participating in the activity. None of the students responded. It was quiet. They seemed to be lost in their own emotions.

I tried again, "How did you feel when the statements were whispered to you? Did you believe them?"

Jamal said something too quietly for me to hear.

Charmiece looked at Jamal and said, "Tell her what you just said."

He looked down and shook his head no.

"You don't want to say?" I asked.

It took everything he had to hold himself together long enough to say, "I believed it when you said it."

For many students (and instructors), this activity is emotionally moving. First-generation, underserved students are often plagued with self-doubt and often question their abilities, their worth, and their aptitude. *Am I good enough? Am I smart enough? Do I have what it takes? No one from my family or my neighborhood makes it out, how can I?* It's sometimes the first time students have heard so many positive things about themselves.

FAMILY AND RELATIONSHIPS

In under-resourced cultures, material possessions are few and resources are scant. However, people are plentiful, and becoming part of a family is more about relationships and less about bloodlines.

When Antoine—a former student—was preparing for the birth of his first child, he asked me to be the baby's Godmother. I was truly honored. I pictured an elaborate church service with everyone dressed in their finest clothes and perhaps a family get-together with a dinner afterward.

After Azariah's birth, I waited patiently for information about the upcoming event, but it never came. There was no event. Eventually, I figured out I officially became her Godmother when it was declared. There was no need for the formality of a church service to coincide with my new title. From that time to this, I'm introduced as "Azariah's Godmother," and I am still involved in her life. We consider each other family.

Fictive kinship is a term that describes kin or social ties that aren't based on blood relations, marriage, or adoption. Students who are "related" through fictive kinship see those "family members" as legitimate relatives.

James H. Whitney III, assistant vice chancellor for undergraduate academic affairs at Rutgers University, stated in his dissertation titled, "Fictive Kin as Capital: A Case Study on African American Youth Aspirations for College":

> These fictive kin relationships may be found in informal structures such as extended family members who are like family but not biologically related, leaders in the community who serve as mentors, precollege encouragement programs, and community and/or religious organizations. Fictive kin relationships serve as alternative family structures that become a form of social and cultural capital necessary for college aspiration in low-income African Americans.

In many cultures, families are made by declaration, "He's my cousin," or "She's my daughter." There are no titles drawing lines of distinction among family members who are not related by blood but are joined by marriage, such as "half-sister" or "step-brother," which seems to be more prevalent among families in privileged cultures.

Faculty who want to engage with students should acknowledge the importance of "family" to these students and recognize that loyalty to "family" extends beyond legal or bloodline relationships.

Family is so highly valued, it often takes precedence over nearly everything, including school. If a student is needed at home to care for a family member—such as a grandparent, parent, sibling or cousin—that's what they will do. A student who has a death in the family may be absent for weeks; they will need to be there to grieve with and support their family. It does not matter if the funeral is four states away and it's the week of exams, they will be gone for as long as necessary to show respect and support for the family. And, they will accept whatever consequence are doled out, including failed classes, loss of financial aid, eviction from campus housing, or dismissal from an athletic team. No price is too high to pay to be with family.

When D'marco lost his cousin, grandmother, and great grandmother in less than two weeks, he left campus and returned home to grieve with his family. D'marco might not have realized how the three weeks away from his classes were going to affect his grades and course completion, but it's unlikely he would have done anything different even if he had known. He had to be there with his family, no matter the consequences.

When D'marco returned to campus, he met with an instructor and asked if he could make up his missed work. The instructor showed little sympathy when D'marco explained his absence. "Everybody dies," the professor said, and added that making up the work wasn't an option.

Rather than being so matter of fact and even cold about D'marco's situation, the professor could have first conveyed sympathy for the student's loss, and then gently explained that it was the policy of the department that assignments and exams could not be made up, regardless the circumstances. It might sound like this, "I'm so sorry to hear about your loss. Please know I will be thinking about you and your family. Unfortunately, I'm not able to allow you to make up the assignments or exams, which will likely negatively impact your final grade in this course. Perhaps you can talk with your advisor about your next steps."

Oftentimes, it's not *what* is said but *how* it's said that makes the difference. If instructors approach situations with care and concern, students are more likely to respond with understanding and appreciation than with anger, frustration, and resentment.

First-generation students often hope that acquiring an education will improve their situation and they will be in the position to help their families financially, especially their parents. Yet, for many, there's also the feeling that success is a long shot and they will never get ahead. Instead of incurring the burden and frustration of trying to plan for upcoming expenses that they know they won't have the funds won't cover, students' solution often seems to be to spend whatever money they have and enjoy today.

Economists Abhijit Banerjee and Esther Duflo, in their book *Poor Economics: A Radical Rethinking of the Way to Fight Global Poverty*, wrote,

"The poor are skeptical about their supposed opportunities, and the possibility of any radical change in their lives…Therefore, they focus on the here and now, on living their lives as pleasantly as possible, and on celebrating when the occasion demands it."

It's also commonplace in under-resourced cultures to share money with family members who are in need. A $500 laptop might be traded for $100 in cash to pay a utility bill. Both parties in the trade believe they have equally benefited; one has electricity, heat, or air conditioning and the other obtained a laptop for practically nothing.

If a student receives bus passes from the student center as a way to get to and from classes, the student will give the passes to the family member who needs transportation to get to work, the grocery store, or laundromat, even if it means the student won't have a way to get to campus.

People who struggle together, who share unpleasant experiences or circumstances, often form a bond. Research published by the Association for Psychological Science (Bastian, Jetten, and Ferris, 2014) suggests that pain may actually serve as a "social glue" that creates solidarity within groups. As a result of shared experiences, it's easy to see how strong bonds develop. Generosity and care are expected. We can see how this plays out among first-generation, marginalized students on campus and in the classroom.

Although these examples are not extreme exaggerations, they are, however, examples of how interdependent cultures, often identified as people having ancestral roots in the Eastern Hemisphere, operate differently from independent cultures, often described as cultures from the Western Hemisphere (Broderick & Blewitt, 2015). Broderick and Blewitt indicate in their text, *The Life Span: Human Development for Helping Professionals*, that to understand cultural differences we must see the world as others do and then we will be able to see differences that "evolved from long histories of practice…" (26). The authors further point out that people from Eastern societies pay attention to the larger context of life in order to thrive by focusing more on interrelationships.

PERCEPTIONS OF TIME

Instructors often interpret students' tardiness to class as laziness or disrespect for the instructor. They might try a variety of ways to modify students' behavior: locking the classroom door at the start of class, taking points away, refusing assignments that were due at the beginning of the class, or electronically locking students out of class message boards or assignment uploads.

However, rather than apathy, disrespect, or indolence, the core of students' time orientation may be based on culture. Philip Zimbardo, a psychologist and professor emeritus at Stanford University, discusses in his YouTube video, "The Secret Powers of Time," the emotional time zones in which people live. He suggests that people who are present-oriented often believe it does not pay to plan, that they believe their life is "fated" by their religion or the circumstances they live under, like poverty. They don't see a reason to plan for the future.

For many economically challenged students, the only thing that matters is what's going on right at that moment. This time orientation is often indirectly modeled and learned in the home. As a result for students who have been raised in low-income households or in under-resourced cultures, the future seems distant and, for the most part, unpredictable. There are so many other more important—sometimes critical—needs requiring attention that planning or preparing for next month, next week, or even tomorrow is not a priority. Students may think, *With all I have going on, it's good enough I show up at all,* or *being a few minutes late is not a big deal.*

College success depends on students' ability to manage their time. This planning may not come naturally for first-generation, marginalized students from under-resourced cultures. It's a skill they need to learn.

One of my students, DeShawn, always arrived to class 15–20 minutes late—sometimes even later. One morning, I asked him to stay after class so I could speak with him. I began, "Thank you for staying after class to talk with me, DeShawn. I notice you sometimes arrive late. Is there anything I can do to help you get here on time?"

DeShawn broke into a broad smile. "Oh, no, Miss Amelia. It's not on you. I just need to get around and get here quicker."

Instructors who want their students to be successful can help by prompting students to schedule study times and due dates in their phones, giving students estimates of how much time an assignment might take to complete, and suggesting when students might begin working on the assignment so it is finished by the due date.

For example, an instructor might say, "You can expect it will take at least two hours for every one typed page. So, if you have a five-page paper due, you can expect it to take 10 hours to complete. Students who want a good grade might want to consider beginning today and plan to work two hours each day until the paper has to be submitted."

EFFORTS AND OUTCOMES

First-generation, marginalized students from under-resourced cultures often believe it's not necessarily their choice how life (or school) will unfold. Ruby Payne, author of *A Framework for Understanding Poverty* wrote, "Individuals in poverty usually have a strong belief in fate and destiny." (661) They believe if it's supposed to work out, it will and if not, it won't. The book has been already written, so to speak. Students who believe their success in life and college is fated also believe their efforts have little to do with their outcomes. They don't bother to put in the time and energy to influence their outcomes, especially if they believe they are already destined to fail. They don't often consider options that might help them to be successful, such as taking fewer credits, getting a tutor, joining a study group, and so on.

A simple conversation that provides options might be all that's needed to help students find alternative ways to continue. On my campus, the sixth week of the semester appears to be a pivotal exit point. Around that time,

I often write a message on the classroom whiteboard (or post online) in large uppercase letters: IF YOU'RE THINKING ABOUT QUITTING, DON'T. TALK TO ME FIRST.

CONFLICT RESOLUTION

In under-resourced cultures, physical dominance and intimidation are seemingly the only ways to resolve conflict, and with few other strategies to rely on, students sometimes bring with them to campus the same problem-solving strategies they have previously used in their neighborhoods, including violence.

Already full of insecurity, self-doubt, and a need to prove oneself, first-generation, underserved students can't allow themselves to be viewed by peers as afraid, weak, or physically unable to defend themselves against a threat. Thinking only of the present, when students are put in positions where they feel they *have* to fight, they will, with little to no consideration of the consequences.

These conflict resolution strategies can be evident in relationships with authority figures as well. A math professor from a community college recently had a student visit his office to discuss his failing grade. The student arrived agitated and things quickly escalated to the point that the faculty member felt threatened and asked the student to leave. When the student blatantly refused, the professor said he, himself, would leave. It was then that the student blocked the door.

Students from under-resourced environments often respond to conflicts in a very spontaneous and direct way. They might not consider walking away, tabling the issue until later, taking some time to cool off, or going to someone for advice before responding. Often, they want to resolve the conflict immediately and sometimes rely on intimidation and physical dominance as a way to come to a resolution. Oftentimes in under-resourced cultures he (or she) who is stronger, bigger, tougher, and louder usually wins.

As with all interactions that could potentially put students in positions to be defensive, delivery is key. To resolve conflict, instructors should remember it's often not *what's* said, but *how* it is said that will determine if the message prompts a response of cooperative action or defensive opposition. Respectful, judgment-free interactions reduce the chance for defensive responses and oppositional behaviors.

To effectively respond to student behaviors in ways that bring cooperation, professors might find it effective to soften their facial expression, shift their body language to a non-aggressive position, and slightly lower the volume of their voice, speaking in a normal, stable, yet gentle tone. Few things will escalate a problem faster than a raised voice. Conversely, speaking quietly often calms tense situations and puts students at ease.

Here are several things to remember when trying to resolve conflict and de-escalate a situation:

- Demonstrate you are on the side of the student.
- Avoid the use of the word *you* which often makes people feel defensive.
- Use the student's name.
- Use *I-statements*.
- Use factual, non-judgmental statements that describe the situation and/or feeling.

Using the scenario previously mentioned with the math professor and student who visited his office to discuss his grade as an example, let's consider how things might have gone differently if the situation played out like this:

The student visits the professor's office to discuss his failing grade. The professor welcomes the student at the door, invites him into his office, and says, "Hi, come in, Terrick. Let's take a look at your grade together and see where things are. Oh, I see where the problem is. It looks like there were two missing assignments and there was a low score on the last quiz."

The professor is mindful not to make the student feel defensive by laying blame or using the word *you*.

The student says, "I tried really hard to do well on that test."

The professor identifies the student's feeling for clarification, "It sounds like you're disappointed in the grade."

The student responds, "I am. I need to pass this class."

The professor uses an *I-statement*, "I understand."

The professor then asks the student questions to show interest and lead the student to a reasonable conclusion: What do you think would be most helpful in preparing for upcoming tests? What needs to happen to be sure all assignments are submitted? What can I do to help you be successful?

The professor welcomed the student, listened, avoided blame and judgment, avoided the word *you*, and showed the student he was on his side. Instead of being the adversarial authority figure, the professor was the supportive ally.

COMMUNICATION

First-generation students, especially students from under-resourced cultures, need to learn how to navigate different environments with different rules. The ways they've interacted and the conversation style they know and have relied on might not work in the higher education arena. Here are some of the communication behaviors that students bring with them to the classroom.

SIMULTANEOUS TALKING

Professors might expect students to be familiar with and conform to a more structured, Eurocentric form of communication that dictates listening without interrupting. This expectation often clashes with the way students from under-resourced cultures engage in communication—they often view this type of discourse as unengaging and banal.

Students who have been raised in under-resourced cultures have learned, mostly through modeling by others, that conversations can include several simultaneous voices. These cultural norms may explain why students might impulsively share their thoughts and comments or engage in side conversations with those around them when professors are lecturing. They also may have learned that communicating effectively means telling the entire story from beginning to end—brevity is neither friendly nor welcoming.

Faculty who show that they are irritated or offended by these students' communication styles inadvertently distance students and shut down engagement, sending a message that not only do they not understand the students' communication style, but also do not value it. This further widens the separation between students and the instructor.

It's important that faculty understand that students who talk when the professor is talking may not necessarily be outwardly disrespecting the instructor. Students might simply be thinking, "Why listen if I can't add to the conversation?"

If side conversations or simultaneous comments are not about the topic at hand, instructors who already have a rapport with students can quickly and easily use an I-statement to redirect students' attention. To ensure order, professors can explain there will be time to listen as well as time to participate in discussion. It might sound like this, "You will have five minutes to discuss the topic in your small groups. Then, we'll reconvene to share thoughts. It's important everyone is heard so when we share out, we'll need it to be quiet enough so everyone can hear the speaker. Today's topic is how cell phone use is linked to brain tumors."

Certainly, instructors can't always allow for participatory group conversation. When that is not an option, the instructor can simply use an I-statement, "I will need it quiet enough that everyone can hear this important information." With relationships and respect in place, a statement like this will be all that's needed.

Quietly asking a student to stay after class to talk privately or giving a student a discreet note during class demonstrates respect, which will certainly be appreciated and reciprocated.

Last fall, there were three young women in my class who were also roommates. They were very comfortable with each other and seemed to bring their lively friendship into the classroom. They sometimes held spirited side conversations when I was teaching. Despite a few respectful strategies I attempted to remediate the issue, their behaviors continued.

One afternoon I discreetly handed each of the three young women a note asking for a conversation after class. The conversation went like this:

Me: I feel like I've been respectful of you.

Student A: Oh, you have. Very much so.

Me: The problem is I don't feel like I'm getting respect in return.

Student A: You're right, you're right. It's just that we're friends and we're just talking.

Student B: We're not trying to be disrespectful.

Me: I understand. When you're talking, though, it's hard for me to be heard. Could you talk to each other after class instead of during class?

All three of the young women agreed they could talk after class. Did their talking stop altogether? Not completely, but things were much better.

VOLUME

In 2016, a group of black women who were on a Napa Valley train to discuss a book and celebrate a birthday were asked by the train staff to quiet down. Ultimately, the train was stopped and the women were escorted by police officers back to the starting point of their trip. Eventually, the CEO of the company publicly apologized and settled with the group, who launched an $11 million lawsuit for racial discrimination, among other charges.

This news story seemed in sharp contrast to a similar story I recently heard from a friend who is white. My friend recounted an experience she had at a local restaurant where she and several of her white, female family members gathered for dinner. It was an especially enjoyable get-together where the women had a spirited conversation. As one story led to the next, their laughter got louder and louder. Interestingly, their experience was very different from that of the black women on the Napa Valley train. Not one, but two customers approached my friend and her family to make comments about how they wished they could have that much fun with their own families.

In the Napa Valley train scenario, it's clear that bias influenced the train's staff to notice the women, interpret the volume of their voices as being too loud, and make the decision to stop the train and call authorities. Similar biases can be present in college classrooms.

Even professors who would not consider themselves biased toward any student groups might demonstrate implicit bias (subconscious) by focusing attention, thoughts, attitudes, and responses to certain groups of students.

For example, if white professors aren't aware of their biases toward students of color, they might not realize they are more prone to pay attention to the volume of their voices and interpret their voices as louder than those of other students.

Additionally, professors sometimes mistakenly believe students who are "being loud" are being purposefully disrespectful. In actuality, the volume of voice is more likely associated with location and culture than disrespect. Results of a study published in *Environmental Health Perspectives* indicate that neighborhoods with higher poverty rates and higher proportions of black, Hispanic, and Asian residents have higher noise levels than other neighborhoods (Casey, Morello-Frosch, Mennitt, et al, 2017), which might influence people from under-resourced areas to talk louder to be heard.

Professors will benefit from examining their biases, thoughts, and beliefs in regard to the volume of students' voices and observing multiple student groups (racial, gender, economic, etc.) to be sure the same standards are in place for all students. When it's valid and necessary to remind students to speak in lower volumes so the professor can be heard, here are some ways to encourage cooperation:

- Communicate only with the student(s) who need a reminder instead of with the students who are close in proximity and may or may not be speaking too loud for the environment.
- Communicate with the student in a way that is as nonpublic as possible. For example, consider using a written message on a small piece of paper that includes an I-statement, and discretely handing it to the student, "I need the volume to come down so everyone can hear the material. Thank you."

TEACHING STUDENTS THE SKILLS

The beginning of a new term is a good time to explain that college is about more than just learning content. It is also about learning different perspectives, considering new ideas, and growing as students, people, and professionals. To do that, students need to be willing to listen attentively to others, be respectful of others, and adhere to the rules of the classroom.

Teaching students how to have appropriate discourse and interactions that encourage mature, effective communication and giving them strategies to engage in conversation with conflicting views is critical. A professor might say, "While you're in college, you will be exposed to controversial topics, new ideas, and new perspectives that you may or may not agree with. You might have strong feelings about these topics that you might want to share. Here are a few ways to disagree respectfully: 'I understand your view. This is how I feel about the topic...' or 'That's an interesting perspective. I have a different viewpoint. I believe...'"

At the same time, it's important that professors understand the characteristics and behaviors discussed in this chapter and use that understanding to support each student.

UNDERSTANDING THE STUDENT EXPERIENCE: ARMANDO'S STORY

THE IMPORTANCE OF SUPPORTIVE RELATIONSHIPS

In under-resourced cultures, living arrangements, utilities, transportation, and food come and go; sometimes you have it and sometimes you don't. But someone is always there for you (your people: family, friends, and neighbors). Without them, first-generation, marginalized students from under-resourced cultures can feel lost and alone.

Armando attended every class and sat in the front row. But rather than paying attention, he would put his head down on the desk and sleep through until dismissal. One day after class I used an I-statement to get the conversation started, "I notice you've been sleeping a lot in class. Is everything ok?"

"Yeah, I'm just tired," he answered.

I pressed on, noticing even his walk looked tired, "It looks like you're really struggling."

"Yeah, I don't know. I just feel so tired all the time," he explained.

"Where are you from, Armando?"

"Wisconsin."

"You're pretty far away from home. You're not homesick, are you?"

"I want to go home really bad…"

"I'm sorry you're struggling, Armando."

"You know, I think I could make it if I could just stay in your class the whole time I'm in college."

Armando's class naps could have been perceived as a disinterest for the content, lack of care about his education or future, or an opportunity to make up lost sleep from social activities from the night before, but Armando was struggling. He missed his family—his people and felt uncomfortable, disconnected, and possibly depressed.

Two weeks later he dropped out and went back to Wisconsin.

REFERENCES

Banerjee A. & Duflo E. *PoorEconomics: A Radical Rethinking of the Way to Fight Global Poverty*. New York: PublicAffairs. 2012.

Bastian B., Jetten J., & Ferris L. Pain as social glue: Shared pain increases cooperation. *Psychological Science* 25(11). 2014: 2079-2085.

Bowerman, Mary. Black women kicked off Napa Valley Wine Train settle, USA TODAY Network. https://www.usatoday.com/story/money/nation-now/2016/04/20/black-women-kicked-off-napa-valley-wine-train-settle-racial-discrimination-case/83280120/. April 20, 2016.

Broderick, P. C., & Blewitt, P. *The life span: Human development for helping professional*. 4th ed. Upper Saddle River, NJ: Pearson. 2015:26

Casey J., Morello-Frosch R., Mennitt D., Fristrup K., Ogburn, E. & James P. "Race/Ethnicity, socioeconomic status, residential segregation, and spatial variation in noise exposure in the contiguous United States. *Environmental Health Perspectives*." https://www.ncbi.nlm.nih.gov/pmc/articles/PMC5744659. July 25, 2017.

Payne, Ruby K. *A Framework for Understanding Poverty: A Cognitive Approach*. 6th ed. aha! Process, Inc.; Sixth Edition. 2018:661.

Whitney, James H. III. "Fictive Kin as Capital: A Case Study on African American Youth Aspirations for College." (Dissertation, Rutgers University, 2016) https://rucore.libraries.rutgers.edu/rutgers-lib/49899/PDF/1/play. 2016.

CHAPTER 4
USING PRACTICAL STRATEGIES TO PROMOTE STUDENT SUCCESS

A central issue in student engagement and success is equitable campus and classroom policies, approaches, and resources. Equity does not mean treating all students the same—a common misconception. Equity does not mean making sure everyone has the same book—it means making sure everyone has what he or she needs.

College professionals can foster equity in the classroom by developing rapport with students, promoting a sense of belonging in the classroom, helping students disrupt long-standing solutions they have relied on to solve problems, reducing and preventing students' self-sabotaging behaviors, and responding and engaging with students in respectful, compassionate, and effective ways.

To make sure classes are equitable, instructors can first focus on developing a welcoming atmosphere for students, especially for first-generation, marginalized students who might feel out of place in the college classroom, particularly if the campus is a predominately white institution.

When working with first-generation, marginalized students, it's important to know that in general:

- They do not want to be put on the spot, called out, or called on.
- Their greatest fear is looking stupid.
- Sarcasm makes them feel stupid even if they seem to "understand" that type of humor.
- Not knowing what to do makes them uncomfortable.
- If they think they are bothering an instructor with questions, they won't ask any.

CARING AND DEVELOPING RAPPORT

Developing rapport with students is one of the most proactive and effective ways to reduce and prevent students' self-sabotaging behaviors and promote success. Caring about students is at the core of developing rapport.

In his 2009 article "Do Your Students Care Whether You Care About Them?" Roosevelt University Professor of Psychology Amere A. Meyers discusses the impact caring for students has on effective college teaching. Meyers states, "Professors do not necessarily prioritize the relationship aspect of teaching to the same extent that learners do." He asserts this is the case even though studies show that students are acutely aware of whether their professors care about them.

Meyers goes on to say that "caring for students is not necessarily an easy task. Some faculty members do care, but feel as though their students do not notice or appreciate their efforts. Other professors feel that it could be too difficult to create caring relationships in large classes or fear that they will be too permissive if they connect with their students. Still others believe that caring is not a part of their job and that focusing on interpersonal relationships at the college level is soft or gratuitous. Although these sentiments are commonly held, they undermine instructional effectiveness."

When considering the cultures and experiences of many first-generation, marginalized students who place a high value on social groups such as family and friends, it makes sense that the key to reducing and preventing education-sabotaging behaviors is to focus on relationships with and among students.

Even professors who understand that relationships are critical to effective teaching and student success wonder how to establish rapport with first-generation students from under-resourced cultures while maintaining a position of esteem and respect as a professor.

GREET AND WELCOME.

The first day of the semester is an ideal time to begin building rapport with students.

A warm greeting and handshake at the classroom door gives students a personal welcome and sets a pleasant, caring tone for the semester ahead. "Welcome to Economics 140. You're in the right place. Glad you're here."

KNOW STUDENTS' NAMES.

Knowing and using students' names is an important part of relationship building. It is the first action that acknowledges students as an individual person and tells them they are important enough to be remembered. "I know who you are. You are somebody to me." Instructors should know students' names and use them both in and out of class.

Here are some tips for remembering/using students' names:

- Use folded pieces of cardstock for name tents for the first few weeks of the semester until names are committed to memory. In larger classes, in lecture halls for example, name tents can be used the entire semester.
- Clarify the pronunciation of students' names if they are unique or have an unusual spelling.
- After learning the name, use it as quickly as possible. "You're Deontaye, right?" or "Welcome, James!"

- Associate the name with a physical reminder. For example, Greg wears glasses or Roderick likes to wear the color red.
- Learn something about the students (their program of study, athletic involvement, place of employment, etc.). We remember students' names when we know something about them as people.
- If you forget a student's name, admit forgetting and ask for a reminder rather than not using the student's name at all. "I'm sorry. I know who you are and that you're in my class but I can't think of your name right now."

When instructors know students' names, students feel visible. It lets them know the instructor took the time to note who they are and considers the students important enough to be remembered.

KNOW STUDENTS AS PEOPLE.

Professors can develop rapport with students by simply communicating with them about their lives and knowing who they are as people. San Diego State University faculty members J. Luke Wood, Frank Harris III, and Khalid White, authors of *Teaching Men of Color in the Community College*, state, "Getting to know students on a personal level will often entail conversations that fall outside the normal academic discourse about grades, course performance, and major choice. Instead, personal conversations should focus on the student as a unique individual who is worthy of the faculty member's attention."

Professors also can let students know they are valued by distributing a letter to students during the first week of the semester introducing themselves and welcoming students to their classes. The letter can share what they enjoy about their content area, why they enjoy teaching, changes they anticipate in their content area, and maybe even a quote they find especially meaningful. At the end of the letter, professors can invite students to write a letter in return that includes specific items they'd like the students to address. For example, they might ask students about their program of study, how they would describe themselves as students, commitments they have outside class, what they value, and quotes they find especially meaningful. Faculty can return the student letters to them with comments and/or questions in the margins, letting students know they took time to read the letters and learn about the students as individuals.

When professors are familiar with the lives of their students, they can inquire about their progress, challenges, and successes. They also can weave references to students' goals or interests openly in the classroom. An instructor might say, "There's a speaker on campus this afternoon who will be discussing social media marketing strategies. D'marco and Jamal, you are both interested in business strategies, you might want to check it out." These types of statements make it clear the professor is interested in their lives and has taken time to get to know them.

AVOID JUDGMENT, CRITICISM, AND DISRESPECT.

Instructors who believe in hierarchal levels that position students at the bottom threaten the learning environment and the opportunity for mutual respect and engaged learning. If students believe they are being judged for their intelligence, neighborhoods, family, culture, sexual orientation, race, or any other characteristic, they will distance themselves from the professor and possibly the class.

First-generation, marginalized student populations are often in a fragile, uncertain state, especially during their first and second years of college. Although filled with optimism, they are unsure about their own abilities to succeed and are often skeptical about the reality of a payoff from a degree that seems out of reach. These students are often one negative event away from walking out of the classroom door. An instructor's sharp, judgmental, or disrespectful response about arriving late to class, sarcastic inquisition about not handing in an assignment, or off-handed comment about not having materials for the course might be just enough to confirm students' feelings that they do not belong and cause them to rethink their commitment to higher education.

Everyone wants to be respected, instructors and students alike. The way to get respect is to give it—by discussing issues privately, addressing behaviors discretely, and treating others as you would like to be treated. As author and poet Maya Angelou stated, "At the end of the day, people won't remember what you said or did, they will remember how you made them feel."

DEMONSTRATE CARE.

Caring shows value and investment. When professors know students' names, inquire about students' progress, and provide students with positive feedback, they are demonstrating care. Because first-generation, marginalized students place a high value on relationships, they are more likely to engage and work to succeed if they believe their teacher knows their needs and cares about them (Rivera-McCutchen, 2012). Here are some ways professors can demonstrate care for students:

- Know students' names.
- Inquire about students' progress.
- Provide students with timely feedback about assignments or grades.
- Use inspiring quotes, written and verbal prompts, guest speakers, or inspirational videos to remind students of the value of education.
- Have a conversation with students about getting back on track when they are not doing well in class. When professors don't address issues, it might be interpreted that they don't care.
- Provide written or verbal motivating retention statements at pivotal exit points, such as "Stay with me, we're almost there. Imagine yourself walking across the stage and having the president of the college hand you your diploma. Your friends and family will be so proud;" "If you are thinking of quitting don't. Talk to me first;" and "You can see the finish line — don't quit now."

- Include inspiring and motivating quotes in the syllabi.
- Get to know students as people, engaging with them in class, responding promptly to students' questions both in and out of class, demonstrating empathy for their struggles and advocating for their success.

Students who believe their instructors sincerely care about them are more likely to put forth effort in the class, engage, cooperate, show respect, persist, and succeed academically.

In every type of communication with students, whether it's face-to-face, handwritten, or electronic, its important instructors first acknowledge the challenges students face as well as the students' feelings about the challenges before moving to the business of the course. Consider the following unedited interactions between students and instructors.

Jada

Jada is clearly overwhelmed and pleading for clemency as well as negotiating a way to stay afloat. The instructor begins by addressing the student's struggle and feelings and demonstrates care by inquiring about the student's safety.

The instructor empathizes with the student, lets the student know about upcoming quizzes and appears to maintain the relationship with the student. Notice, however, the instructor doesn't approve the absences nor accept the offer of an additional 4-page paper.

Jada

Thu 3/17/2016 10:26 AM

Hello I talked to you Tuesday but it's seems like every since my mom gotten sick I have been having nothing but bad luck I had an accident on the way to school this morning so that's how come I wasn't in class all I keep doing is crying because I have been trying so hard and I hope you understand that i haven't just been missing class it's not like that

at all my mom is still not great and by me being the only child home I can't help it so please please excuse me today I will even write you a 4 page paper and turn it in if that would help me
Sent from Outlook Mobile

Hi Jada,

I'm so sorry to hear you were in an accident. Are you ok? I understand things are difficult right now. Let's talk when you return to class about some possible ways to help you be successful. I announced in class today that we have a vocab quiz Tuesday as well as an in-class, open-book quiz over chapter 8.

Hope this helps.

Malik

Malik kept his email short and to the point to let the instructor know he was ill. The instructor thanks the student for the information about the absence and then demonstrates care by wishing the student well. Finally, with the relationship still intact, the instructor reminds the student about the attendance policy and the total days missed so far in the term.

Malik
Mon 11/30/2015 9:48 AM
Sorry I cannot make it to class today I'm terribly sick

Malik,

Thank you for letting me know you won't be in class today. Hope you're feeling better soon. Please refer to the syllabus to review the class attendance policy. Keep in mind that grades go down .5 (half a grade) each time you are absent. So far, you have missed 7 days of class.

Brittney

Brittney explains her absence and requests making up the day's assignment. The instructor demonstrates care for the student with empathic response and get-well wishes. Even though the instructor refuses Brittney's request to make up the assignment, Brittney's reply indicates the relationship is maintained.

Brittney
Thu 3/17/2016 9:58 AM
Good morning I'm just now waking up I was meaning to email you last night. I wasn't able to make it to class because I don't feel good at all, I believe I have either a 24-hour virus or food poisoning if there is anyway I could make up today's work may I please!

Hi Brittney,
I'm sorry to hear you're not feeling well. Hope you feel better soon. Unfortunately, in-class work, quizzes and assignments can't be made up. I announced in class today that we have a vocab quiz Tuesday. Hope this helps.

Brittney
Thank you so much!

Relationship building is based on care, and caring is often reciprocal. When instructors demonstrate care, students usually reciprocate. When instructors show sincere concern about students' lives and progress, then students are also often more apt to rise to the instructors' expectations and are more motivated to achieve goals even when they have encountered previous and consistent challenges.

ASSUME POSITIVE INTENT.

Professors sometimes mistakenly assume that negative, unproductive, or impolite student behaviors are a result of students' lack of respect for instructors and/or lack of care about the class, course work, or grades. In reality, students' behaviors might be a response to a lack of resources or inability to manage the college environment, complete work, manage time, meet deadlines, engage with e-class formats, navigate unexpected life events, or manage racial tensions, which are often unnoticed by college faculty and staff

For example, an instructor might conclude that a student did not hand in an assignment because he did not care about the course when in reality, the student might have a deep regard for the class but was unable to meet the deadline because he couldn't get access to a computer, printer, course materials, transportation, or other resources.

If faculty assume students are intentionally trying to disrespect or disrupt their classes, they can become judgmental, limiting expressions of care and compassion, thinking, "Students do not want what I have to offer so I'm not going to waste my time trying to connect."

Conversely, assuming positive intent allows professors to instruct, care, and serve at their fullest potential and keeps them in a place of solutions and service. When instructors assume positive intent, it impacts how they perceive behaviors and how they interact with students and increases the likelihood students will engage and become empowered to succeed.

Research indicates that first-generation students value education, want to do well in college, and often see it as their ticket to a better life. How different the class culture would be if instructors embraced the idea that students wanted and intended to do well and are doing the best they can with the resources, information, and experiences they have.

DEVELOP CLASS COMMUNITY.
Instructors must not only develop relationships *with* students, they must also facilitate relationships *among* students. Developing a community within a class fosters a sense of unification, belongingness, collaboration, and support that many students, especially first-generation, marginalized students, need in order to feel welcome and comfortable.

It's not unusual for college students to struggle with loneliness, especially students from urban areas who are accustomed to being within walking distance of stores, food trucks, bus stops, clinics, and community agencies. Friends, family, and extended family, too, are often only blocks away. Students from urban areas often find themselves distant from social support systems and struggle with feelings of homesickness, boredom, isolation, and anxiety in their new environments and would likely benefit from a sense of belonging in the classroom. Here are some ways to encourage class community:

Don't require students to speak in front of the class. Expecting first-generation students to be comfortable enough in their new surroundings in the first few weeks to introduce and talk about themselves can be overwhelming.

Some professors rationalize that many students will have to speak publicly in their future jobs and the sooner they learn to be comfortable with it, the better, so they require their students to speak in front of the class during the first week of the term—sometimes the first day.

Many students, especially first-generation, marginalized students, might not be ready to speak in a new environment where they might already feel ill-equipped and out of place. Understanding and respecting students' feelings and fears and scaffolding their learning is another way to foster rapport with students. Professors can begin each semester by telling students they recognize that not everyone is comfortable speaking aloud and there are many other options available to share views without speaking publicly. Options might include having students talk in small groups of three or four, having classmates who are bold speak on the behalf those who are bashful, and using technology such as Socrative or Poll Everywhere that allows students to provide anonymous but public feedback that's displayed in real time.

Encourage community and sense of belonging. One of the best ways to get people to bond is to have them work together to meet a common goal. Group activities are an effective way for building community in the classroom. Some of the most effective community-building activities include clear directions, student interaction, movement, and opportunities for students to reveal something about themselves (their hometown, program of study, hobbies, etc.).

Professors who replace the words *I*, *you*, and *your* with *our*, *we*, and *us* intentionally—yet subtly—encourage a sense of community and belonging in the classroom. Inclusive words let students know they are a part of a group, a classroom community that has a common experience and goal.

For example, the instructor might say, "Let's look at the criteria for *our* next assignment," instead of, "You need to look at the criteria for your next assignment." This simple, consistent change in language sends the message the instructor and the class belong to the same collective group with the same goal.

Share stories. Storytelling is a way to communicate and connect. Stories build relationships because by sharing something about ourselves we demonstrate that we're willing to let others know us. When instructors share stories with students about challenges and accomplishments against the odds, students know instructors understand the difficulties they are facing and have a sense of hope that they, too, will prevail. Stories instructors share should be brief, real, and truthful. The stories need to be relevant to the students' lives or experiences. Here's an example story I often share with students:

When I started college, I went on the buddy system. My friend, Phyllis and I (who were both first-generation students) decided it would be easier if we took classes together, that way we wouldn't feel so alone. It was the perfect plan; we could ride to campus together, attend class and do homework together, and support each other.

The first semester went pretty well and we both passed our classes.

But, my friend decided it wasn't a good time for her to be in school and quit after our first semester. When I had to continue on my own, I felt more alone than ever, but I kept going. Things went well for a while, but eventually the stress of trying to navigate college and life caught up with me, too.

One day, Phyllis stopped by, and as we talked I started crying. I was completely overwhelmed. I told her I was struggling and didn't know how I was going to be able to continue.

She listened carefully and then asked, "What's really the problem?"

I explained that I just couldn't keep up with everything: my classes, homework, trying to find time to sleep, working, paying my bills, everything. It was then that she told me I had come too far and that I couldn't quit. I had to keep going.

Phyllis was a waitress at a local restaurant and bar. After getting permission from the owner, she took on an extra day of work each week and set the tips aside from her extra shift. At the end of the month, she took the tips from her extra day and made my monthly car payment. This went on for a full year. Yes, you heard me correctly—she worked an extra day each week for a year to pay my car payment so I could stay in school.

Now, you might be thinking 'she had the money and it wasn't a sacrifice to make the payment,' but there's nothing further from the truth. She and her husband were raising two young children and living week-to-week just like the rest of us. She literally took time and money away from her own family to help me make it through school. Phyllis never was able to go back to school, and to this day she continues to work at the same restaurant. Instead of feeling jealous or envious that I went on and received my degree, she unselfishly supported and encouraged me.

That is the kind of friend you need to have around you. The friends that are trying to pull you away—to the club, to a party, to a movie, when they know you are trying to get through school—are not helping you get where you're going.

Now might be the time to put some temporary distance between yourself and those who are moving in a different direction. Be careful not to leave them behind, though. Plan to rejoin them when you are on solid ground.

Stories allow students to see professors as real people who have struggled and overcame challenges.

Motivate and inspire. First-generation, underserved students from under-resourced cultures need to see incremental successes and hear messages of encouragement along the way. Professors demonstrate care when they intentionally motivate and inspire students to keep going, even when things get hard. Students know professors care about them when professors take time to tell stories of triumph, share uplifting quotes, show motivating TedTalks, and play video clips from motivational speakers. Professor can also weave messages of motivation into syllabi, including inspirational quotes from remarkable people who demonstrated tenacity and overcame struggles, such as Tupac Shakur, Albert Einstein, Rosa Parks, Bill Gates, Oprah Winfrey, Frederick Douglass, and many others.

RESPONDING TO UNPRODUCTIVE AND NEGATIVE BEHAVIORS

Each semester, I include an attendance and tardy policy in my syllabi. I also make it a point on the first day of class to explain the importance of consistent attendance and being on time, and the potential disruption of late arrival to class. I tell students it's especially important to arrive to class on time on quiz days, as it's my practice to allow students the first 10 minutes of class to review notes before the quiz.

James, a first-generation student who lived on campus, attended our 9:00 a.m. class nearly every day but consistently arrived anywhere from 10 to 20 minutes *after* class began.

On the day of our first vocabulary quiz, I handed out the quiz at 9:10 a.m. At 9:20, James arrived and headed toward his usual seat.

I greeted James as he sat down and handed him the quiz. The look on his face told me he forgot it was a quiz day. As I quietly moved around the room, I watched James put his book bag on his lap and begin to slowly rifle through it, pretending to search for a pen while trying to look at the vocabulary definitions in his open bag.

I walked over to James and when his eyes met mine, I spoke quietly so other students wouldn't hear, "How about I take your quiz back and give you some time to look over your notes? Then, when you're ready, give me a signal and I'll bring the quiz back for you to complete."

He said nothing, but nodded. I took the quiz and placed it on my desk and after a few minutes, he let me know he was ready.

Nobody likes to be called out in front of their peers, especially first-generation, underserved students who are often filled with self-doubt and uncertainty about their ability to be successful. When student behaviors need to be addressed, students are more likely to cooperate when professors communicate with care and respect, privately and discretely.

DON'T USE PUNISHMENT TO CHANGE BEHAVIOR.
Punishing students by embarrassing them, calling them out, or shaming them will not bring about change.

For example, if a student arrives late to class and the professor thinks, "Oh, I'll fix them. I'll lock the door so they can't get in. I'll bet they find a way to make it to class on time next week," the instructor's efforts to bring about change will be in vain. The only thing that will change will be the size of the wedge that's driven between the instructor and the student.

A statement on The National Association of School Psychologist website seems to be on the mark: "Punishment often fails to stop, and can even increase the occurrence of the undesired response." Professors can promote success by talking respectfully with students about unproductive behaviors and offering alternative approaches. In that way, relationships are maintained or perhaps even strengthened, and everyone moves on, unscathed.

REMEMBER THAT STUDENT BEHAVIORS ARE NOT PERSONAL.

Most often, student behaviors have very little to do with professors or other college professionals and are, instead, ways the students are trying to solve their own problems. When instructors personalize student behaviors, they often come from a place of frustration and fear and respond in ways that are disproportionate to the situation. When that happens, professors lose credibility and create an environment that is at odds with students rather than in partnership with them. When professors let go of the idea that disruptive behaviors are personal affronts and instead considering what is driving students' behaviors, professors are more likely to engage with students in compassionate ways that lead students to success.

STAY CALM.

When instructors become openly irritated, frustrated, or angry it often invokes a more aggressive response from students. Instructors should not let students see them rattled no matter how frustrated or angry. When instructors come from a place of anger or fear they have already lost.

USE I-STATEMENTS.

The word *you* can make routine comments and questions seem judgmental and put students on the defensive, which frequently requires a self-justifying or self-protecting response. When interacting with students, instructors might find it more productive and less accusatory to use I-statements.

Andrew Dlugan, professional blogger and founder of Six Minutes, a public speaking and presentation website, says that when the word *you* is used, the unspoken message being received is, "Hrumph! They don't care about the problem...they are just trying to pin the blame on me!" Dlugan suggests placing the focus on the action, task, or entity involved.

When instructors use I-statements, they own the experiences they are having with the students instead of making a personal judgment about the students' behaviors. For example, an instructor might receive better results that promote student success by saying, "I didn't receive your assignment," instead of, "You didn't hand in your assignment." Or, an instructor might say, "I noticed the deadline was missed," instead of, "Why did you miss the deadline?" Although the example sentences say the same thing, removing the word *you* reduces the potential for students to feel defensive. Here are a few more examples:

- "I notice there's been some difficulty arriving to class on time. Is everything ok?"
- "I haven't received the assignment. Do you have any unanswered questions?"
- "I hear some side conversations."

MAKE EYE CONTACT.
Many times, misbehavior will dissipate with a simple look from the professor. The "look" shouldn't be threatening or aggressive but should convey the idea, "I see it and that behavior isn't helping you get where you want to go."

ROAM THE ROOM AND KEEP CLOSE PROXIMITY.
Faculty who avoid staying at the front of the classroom and instead move around while teaching, lingering near disengaged students, are more likely to hold the attention of their students and encourage their engagement.

USE "HOW-CAN-I-HELP-YOU?" QUESTIONS.
Most first-generation, underserved students do the work if they have the resources and know how to do it. The problem arises when they don't have the materials they need (e-devices, textbooks, calculators, etc.), feel the work is too difficult or overwhelming, or they don't know where to start. Professors can help by asking questions such as:

- "How can I help you get started with the assignment?"

- "How can I help you prepare for the quiz?"
- "How can I help you get to class on time?"
- "How can I help you be more engaged?"

Keep in mind, students do not want to reveal they are having problems to those they do not know, trust, or respect, especially if their problems are related to money.

ALLOW MISTAKES.

In his book *The Beautiful Struggle*, Ta-Nehisi Coates lets his son know that because he is human, he will make mistakes. Coates writes, "You will misjudge. You will yell. You will drink too much. You will hang out with people you shouldn't. Not all of us can always be Jackie Robinson – not even Jackie Robinson was always Jackie Robinson. But the price of error is higher for you than it is for your countrymen . . ."

The absence of equity can often be seen in K-12 classrooms, communities, society, and court rooms where marginalized students have already lived the higher "price of error" to which Coates refers. Instructors have an opportunity to write a new script, allowing students' mistakes, decisions, and behaviors to be temporary; forgiving whatever infraction occurred and beginning again with a clean slate.

SAY SOMETHING.

Professors need to care enough to say something to students when they are not doing well. For example, if professors notice students are absent, coming late, not studying, or failing, they should have a courageous conversation with the students. Having an honest conversation about students' progress demonstrates care. Silence means students are invisible and there has been no notice or concern about their struggles.

UNDERSTANDING THE STUDENT EXPERIENCE: DARRIAN'S STORY

CARING AND DEVELOPING RAPPORT

While at the white board I was writing sentence starters to prompt responses for a reflection paper:

I learned . . .

I discovered . . .

I was surprised by . . .

I already new . . .

Darrian remarked, "You spelt a word wrong."

"I did? Where?" I said as I stepped back from the board to review my work.

"Right there. You wrote *n-e-w*. *Knew* is spelt with a *k*, *k-n-e-w*."

"Touché," I conceded. "You are correct," I said as I squeezed a slightly crooked *k* in front of the *n*.

However, when I turned my back to the class to finish writing the prompts on the board I heard Darrian whisper a comment under his breath, "Maybe you the one that needs an English class."

I turned around and looked, expressionless, at Darrian.

Jala who was seated in front of him looked appalled. "Did you hear what he just said?" she asked me.

"I did." I said matter of factly.

Jala turned to Darrian, and said. "You rude. Look what you said to her."

I interrupted, "No worries, Jala. I didn't take what Darrian said personally because he didn't mean it that way, did you, Darrian?" Although

I was talking to Jala my eyes never left Darrian.

The class watched and listened for his response but he didn't answer. He just looked at me. He didn't confirm, nor deny, my implication of unintentional disrespect.

I resumed my attention to the board, class proceeded and we moved on.

Later, as students packed up their things and moved to dismiss, I asked Darrian to stay after class for a couple minutes. When the last student left class, he approached the front of the room where I was standing.

"Tuesday you said you had a problem and you'd take care of it. I didn't hear from you, so I took care of it for you." Then, I handed him the bag of groceries I had concealed under my coat that was on chair.

For a few seconds, that seemed longer than it really was, he said nothing. He just looked at me.

On the previous day of class, moments before the other students arrived Darrian mentioned he was "so hungry." When I inquired about his campus meal card, he said he had used it all during the first month of the term. When I asked how he'd been eating for the past couple months he said he "gets along" by asking random students for one meal off their campus meal card.

Darrian, who was miles away from his home in Detroit, had no car, no money, no food, and no family support. His father is serving life without parole. His brother, too, is currently incarcerated.

REFERENCES

Dlugan, Andrew. "Defensive Reponses: Not 'Why', but 'You.'" Six Minutes Presentation website. http://sixminutes.dlugan.com/ defensive-reponses-not-why-but-you. November 28, 2007.

Coates, T. *The Beautiful Struggle: A Memoire.* New York: Spiegel & Grau. 2008:95

Meyers, SA. "Do your students care whether you care about them?" *College Teaching,* 57 (4). 2009:205-210.

Rivera-McCutchen, RL. "Caring in a small urban high school: A complicated success." *Urban Education,* 47(3). 2012:653-680.

Wood J., Harris F., & White K. *Teaching Men of Color in the Community College: A Guidebook.* San Diego: Montezuma Publishing. 2015:41.

CHAPTER 5
LOOKING WITHIN

People oftentimes believe their emotions, especially negative emotions such as anger, fear, frustration, and disappointment, are caused by outside influences such as other people, events, or situations.

For example, a professor might think his/her anger and frustration is caused by a student's habitual late arrival, "That student is late *again*! I'm tired of seeing her saunter in 15 minutes late and disrupting class! She is so inconsiderate." However, it could be that the professor's anger and frustration stems from what he's thinking about the *student* instead of the student's late arrival.

Epictetus, a Greek philosopher and Roman slave, explained it this way, "Men are disturbed not by things, but by the view which they take of them." How we *think* of things influences how we feel and react. Thoughts as well as actions are based on what we think and believe. It's important professors and other college professionals explore what they *think* of students' behaviors and how their perceptions might impact how they engage with students.

Cognitive Behavior Therapy (CBT) is a therapeutic approach used to help understand how thoughts, attitudes, and beliefs affect decisions and actions. Briefly, here's how CBT works: An event happens (activating event) that triggers thoughts and feelings that are based on beliefs. Thoughts and feelings cause people to take action. Actions spur outcomes (consequences).

Professors can use a CBT approach to examine their thoughts, attitudes, and beliefs to understand the decisions they make and the actions they take when engaging with first-generation, marginalized students from under-resourced cultures and the outcomes their actions yield.

Let's use a CBT approach to explore a classroom scenario that was referenced in Chapter 1. (Visit this link to view the video: https://www.youtube.com/watch?v=v2AmSMnAyeA.)

An intense in-class clash took place between a professor and a student that appeared to start from a dispute over an incorrect answer to an assignment or quiz question. The professor in the video seemed to believe the student's behavior was disruptive, obstinate, threatening, and combative. The student appeared to believe her own behaviors and responses were justified and warranted and even stated the instructor was arguing with her and making her "get more uncomfortable and angry." The student ultimately refused the professor's request to leave the classroom and was eventually physically removed by campus security.

Using a CBT approach, it's necessary to first identify the **activating event**. The activating event can be any situation or experience that prompts an emotional or behavioral response. Many times, the activating event will be the last straw, so to speak, that occurs right before the emotional or behavioral response. In this scenario, the activating event was the student's refusal to leave the classroom. The activating event triggers the professor's **thoughts and feelings**, which are based on **beliefs**.

Breaking the Cycle: Basic Cognitive Skills (The Change Companies, 2010) defines beliefs in this way: "Beliefs are the ideas about the world around you and how it operates. This includes your expectations of other people, and the assumptions you make about their thoughts and feelings. It also includes your beliefs about what is right or wrong, or good or bad. Your beliefs are what you say to yourself in your own head (your 'self-talk')."

The only way to accurately know the professor's thoughts and beliefs would be to ask her, but because that's not possible, for this example we will hypothesize her thoughts and beliefs based on her responses as presented in the video. The professor might think, "This student is a troublemaker. I'm frustrated. She doesn't respect me, care about this class, or her education. I'm angry. Her behavior is ruining my class, taking away my teaching time, and undermining my credibility as a professor. She's not college material and doesn't belong in a college class. If she's bold enough to talk to me like this, what else will she do? I'm afraid. She might be dangerous."

The professor's thoughts and feelings, which are based on her beliefs, drive her **action** to call campus security. The professor's emotional responses (thoughts and feelings) might have been feeling fearful, frustrated, and angry as well as powerless—she was unable to get the student under control. The professor's behavioral responses (action) included debating and arguing with the student and calling campus security to have the student physically removed from class.

It might seem the professor in the scenario called campus security because the student "made the professor fearful, frustrated, and angry." The professor's action spurs the **outcome** (or consequence): the student was physically removed from the classroom. Although we don't know for certain, we could also hypothesize additional outcomes occurred such as the student being banned from class or campus, causing her to have a reduction in credits attempted and passed, possibly losing financial assistance, and delaying completion and graduation.

CBT SCENARIO SNAPSHOT

Activating Event: The student refuses to leave the classroom.

Beliefs: "This student is a troublemaker. I'm frustrated. She doesn't respect me, care about this class or her education. I'm angry. Her behavior is ruining my class, taking away my teaching time and undermining my credibility as a professor. She's not college material and doesn't belong in a college class. If she's bold enough to talk to me like this, what else will she do?

I'm afraid. She might be dangerous."

Action: The professor debated and argued with the student. The professor felt powerless; she couldn't get the student under control. The professor called campus security.

Outcomes: The student was physically removed from class.

With the professor's beliefs included in the scenario it's easy to see how her thinking influenced her decision to call campus security to have the student physically removed from class.

ANOTHER PERSPECTIVE

Now, using an empathic, compassionate approach, let's use the same scenario, with the same activating event but with different beliefs to understand how thoughts and feelings impact beliefs, actions, and outcomes that support student success:

Activating Event: The student's refusal to leave the classroom.

Beliefs (based on thoughts and feelings): "The student is a first-generation student. She's living on campus, and she's far away from home. She's one of the few marginalized students in my class. She might feel like an outsider. She might be afraid of failing, afraid of looking weak in front of her peers, afraid of being powerless. I don't think she feels safe. Her experiences might tell her not to trust authority figures. As an educator, *I* am an authority figure."

Action: The professor engages with the student with understanding, compassion, and empathy: "I'd like to see you be successful. Let's spend some time after class so I can better answer your question," or "It sounds like this is really important to you. I'm sure we can work this out. Let's look at this together after class."

Outcome: The student believes the professor is on her side and wants her to be successful. The student is satisfied and agrees to meet with the professor. The professor has maintained a relationship with the student and moves on with the class lecture.

In the first example, an intense dispute occurred that resulted in the student being physically removed from class. If the student is allowed back in the class, the professor will have to work hard to repair the relationship with the student in order for the student to be successful.

In the second example, the professor manages her discomfort with the student's behaviors and engages with the student with compassion and empathy, maintains the relationship, and lets the student know that she understands and is on her side. The professor behaves in a way that supports student success.

FINDING PERSPECTIVE

Professors' thoughts and feelings, which are based on their beliefs about students, determine their responses because their thoughts and feelings come from what they believe to be true. Here are some questions that can help professors manage their thinking about student behavior:

- Are your beliefs and thoughts coming from a place of compassion and empathy?
- Are your beliefs and thoughts helping you build and maintain relationships with students?
- Are your beliefs and thoughts getting the outcomes you want for your students and yourself?
- Are your beliefs and thoughts helping support student success?

The immediate benefit of a compassionate, empathic approach is that it de-escalates situations. Responding and engaging with students in empathic and compassionate ways will bring better outcomes, building upon relationships instead of dismantling them.

A compassionate, empathic approach takes consistency and time, and professors should avoid thinking, "I tried it once and it did not work." Each time professors show respect, kindness, compassion, and empathy toward students, it's like money in the bank. They're building capital in the way of trust, cooperation, engagement, and student success.

UNDERSTANDING THE STUDENT EXPERIENCE: ISAIAH'S STORY

MAKING A CONNECTION

It's important first-generation, marginalized students from under-resourced cultures feel they're not alone and that someone is in their corner. It has been suggested that if students are connected to at least one person on campus they are more likely to persist. Isaiah struggled to stay afloat in his classes because he did not have any of the textbooks. He had received financial aid, but there wasn't enough left over to purchase books and materials. He was having an especially hard time in his business class.

As a facilitator of the campus African-American male success initiative, I was invited to an appointment with Isaiah and his business instructor to discuss his missing assignments.

A couple days later, I checked in with Isaiah, and he said things were getting better but he had another assignment due that again, required the textbook. I told Isaiah I thought all the textbooks were available in the library for students to check out.

Isaiah and I walked to the library and talked with the woman behind the desk who confirmed the textbooks were there. Isaiah requested the book he needed, but his library card was declined because there was a balance from late fees.

"Isaiah really needs this book. Is there any way he can check it out and catch up the late fees at another time?" I pleaded.

"No, the fees need to be paid before he can check out another book."

"I understand. How about this: Can he just use the book here, in the library, not leave with it but just use it here and then give it back to you when he's done?"

"No, he needs to check it out to use it."

"Ok. Could he make a few copies of the pages he needs and then give you back the book?"

"No, he needs to check the book out to be able to use it."

"Isaiah really needs the book to be successful with his assignment. What do I need to do to make sure he can get it?"

"The late fees need to be paid."

I rifled through my teacher bag, found my wallet and pulled out a $20 bill. "Please use this to cover his late fees."

She took the $20, handed me the receipt, and handed Isaiah the book. Isaiah didn't say anything. He just watched the transaction between the library clerk and me, but when we left, he said, "Nobody has ever done anything like that for me before."

"Yeah? Well, it's important you have the book. I want you to do well."

I don't know if Isaiah meant that nobody ever paid a fee for him or that nobody ever advocated for him, but either way he learned I was on his side.

REFERENCE

The Change Companies. *Breaking the Cycle: Basic Cognitive Skills.* Carson City, NV: The Change Companies. 2010:2

CHAPTER 6
FINAL THOUGHTS

Teaching is a human service profession, and those who choose to teach do so because they want to contribute positively to the lives of students. Professors know a college degree is far more than a student's stepping-stone to a profession. As The College Board reported in 2016, a college education is linked to "higher pay, job security, healthier behaviors and more civic involvement."

Colleges have called first-generation, marginalized, and under-resourced students to their campuses, and students have accepted the invitation. However, getting students to register is only the beginning. Once students become a part of the college community, it is the ethical responsibility of the organization as a whole to give students what they need to be supported, safe, and successful.

It would be inequitable as well as professionally neglectful to invite students to register for classes and live on campuses that lack resources, supports, a safe campus culture that values diverse populations, and knowledgeable faculty who are skilled in strategies that help students feel welcomed, understood, and valued. Colleges simply cannot ask students to be a part of a campus community that does not provide them with the tools, resources, and supports they need; that would be setting students up for failure.

If ethical reasons aren't enough to persuade colleges to position themselves to understand, welcome, and support students, perhaps considering the fiscal impact of student attrition will encourage them to take action. It is more beneficial and less expensive to provide supports and resources for students than it is to recruit new students. Additionally, public policy is leaning on colleges to increase completion rates.

Faculty, too, have placed themselves in positions of responsibility for welcoming, understanding, and supporting students by choosing to teach at higher education organizations that have "invited" first-generation, marginalized, under-resourced students to their campuses. Some faculty would argue they don't choose the students in their classes; instead, students simply appear on their class rosters. But faculty have a host of choices in regard to the kind of institutions with which they affiliate and the student populations they encounter.

ONE LAST MESSAGE

Even the most committed professors might find themselves thinking, "College isn't for everyone. If students aren't able and prepared, wouldn't it be easier if I just weed them out in the first week or two? After all, I'm being held accountable for the number of students who pass my classes."

Other professors might wonder, "What's in it for me? How am I going to gain by taking this approach?" Heavy teaching loads, overburdened schedules, and limited time can interrupt abilities to check thoughts, beliefs, attitudes and biases that get in the way of considering responses and strategies that will most encourage student success. When that happens here are some things to keep in mind:

- Students' histories, experiences, values, and cultures might be very different from those of college professionals. It is the responsibility of colleges and professors to become aware of those differences.
- Relationships with and among students are crucial to student engagement and success.
- Students are doing the best they can with the information and

skills and resources they currently have.

- Students' behaviors are rarely personal affronts but instead are long-standing solutions to their own problems.
- An empathic, compassionate approach contributes to the human experience instead of taking away from it.

Students are counting on us, not just to provide them with *opportunities* to succeed but to provide them with a welcoming campus climate and the resources and supports necessary for their success.

Basic psychology tells us when students feel welcome, comfortable, safe, respected, supported, connected, and cared about, they are much more apt to consistently attend class, participate, engage, complete assignments, try harder, study more, and feel an obligation to succeed and not disappoint those they care about including their professors with whom they have a rapport.

REFERENCE

"College Education Linked to Higher Pay, Job Security, Healthier Behaviors and More Civic Involvement: New College Board Report." The College Board website. https://www.collegeboard.org/releases/2016/college-education-linked-to-hgher-pay-job-security-healthier-behaviors-and-more-civic-involvement. January 9, 2017.

ABOUT THE AUTHOR

AMELIA LEIGHTON GAMEL is an assistant professor at Jackson College, where her focus is on equity and inclusion.

The founder of two nationally recognized college success initiatives that promote the success and advancement of African American college students (Men of Merit and Sisters of Strength), she has devoted her career to encouraging student success and assisting faculty in identifying and eliminating barriers that prevent the full participation and success of first-generation, under-resourced, and marginalized student populations.

Gamel's successful leadership in the classroom is a result of her no-nonsense but compassionate methods, her interpersonal skills, her insight into the human experience, and a genuine passion and value for racial and social equity.

She is a national speaker and consultant; the founder of EquitableEDU, LLC, which promotes equity and empowers educators to effectively engage with students

AMELIA LEIGHTON GAMEL

CONNECT WITH AMELIA

🌐 Visit Amelia's webpage: EquitableEDU.org

🐦 Follow Amelia on Twitter @AmeliaGamel

OTHER PUBLICATIONS BY AMELIA LEIGHTON GAMEL

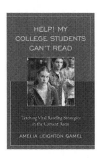

Help! My College Students Can't Read: Teaching Vital Reading Strategies in the Content Areas. Rowman & Littlefield Publishers, 2015.

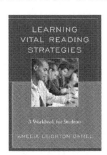

Learning Vital Reading Strategies: A Workbook for Students. Rowman & Littlefield Publishers, 2016.